THE NEW SPIRITUALITY

RUDOLF STEINER

The New Spirituality
and the Christ Experience
of the Twentieth Century

Seven lectures given in Dornach
17 to 31 October 1920

Translated by Paul King

RUDOLF STEINER PRESS LONDON
ANTHROPOSOPHIC PRESS, HUDSON N.Y.

FIRST EDITION 1988

ALL RIGHTS RESERVED
© RUDOLF STEINER PRESS LONDON

ISBN RSP 0 85440 646 8 (HB)
ISBN RSP 0 85440 656 5 (PB)
ISBN AP 0 88010 212 8 (HB)
ISBN AP 0 88010 213 6 (PB)

Edited by John Lees

Printed in Great Britain by Adlard & Sons

CONTENTS

Dornach, 17 October 1920 . . .   7
    Significant moments of world history. Study of the symptoms of history. The dispute around 800 AD concerning the nature of death between the French philosopher Alcuin and a Greek thinker. The influences of oriental spiritual life on the Centre and on the West. Platonism and Aristotelianism. The culture of the East – a decadent spiritual life; the culture of the West – a thinking suited to the economic life; the culture of the Centre – a logical-dialectical-legal thinking occupying itself with what the human being experiences between birth and death and capable of establishing the civic-judicial element. The culture of the 'I'. 'We have arrived at the point of human development at which an understanding for all three areas must spread equally over all humanity.' Spiritual science as an initiate culture is the means and path for this. The need to extend the Free School of Spiritual Science and to establish a World Fellowship of Schools.

Dornach, 22 October 1920 . . .   27
    The development of I-consciousness since the fifteenth century. The threefold principle in the course of history. The elemental beings in the West and the East who oppose the threefold idea.

Dornach, 23 October 1920 . . . 41
> Development in the three streams arising from the decline of Rome. The human being of the Centre between East and West. New economy, static jurisprudence, finished spiritual life.

Dornach, 24 October 1920 . . . 57
> Schiller's *Aesthetic Letters* and Goethe's *Fairy-tale* in their relation to Anthroposophy and the threefold principle.

Dornach, 29 October 1920 . . . 75
> The change in the soul-constitution of humanity since the fifteenth century. The decline in the intensity of knowledge. The emergence of intellectualism and the development of human freedom. The power of intellect and the human longing for knowledge.

Dornach, 30 October 1920 . . . 91
> The development of the perception of Christ from Gnosis up to the present. The church ban on reading the Gospels. The path of Imagination. The reappearance of Christ.

Dornach, 31 October 1920 . . . 107
> The future spiritual battle between the East and the West. The imminent Christ-experience of the twentieth century. The change in humanity's constitution of soul since the fifteenth century.

Notes . . . 124

Dornach, 17 October 1920

In the lectures given here during the course on history[1] several things were mentioned which, particularly at the present time, it is especially important to consider. With regard to the historical course of humanity's development, the much-debated question mentioned to begin with was whether the outstanding and leading individual personalities are the principal driving forces in this development or whether the most important things are brought about by the masses. In many circles this has always been a point of contention and the conclusions have been drawn more from sympathy and antipathy than from real knowledge. This is one fact which, in a certain sense, I should like to mention as being very important.

Another fact which, from a look at history, I should like to mention for its importance is the following. At the beginning of the nineteenth century Wilhelm von Humboldt[2] appeared with a definite declaration, stipulating that history should be treated in such a way that one would not only consider the individual facts which can be outwardly observed in the physical world but, out of an encompassing, synthesizing force, would see what is at work in the unfolding of history – which can only be found by someone who knows how to get a total view of the facts in what in a sense is a poetic way, but in fact produces a true picture. Attention was also drawn to how in the course of the nineteenth century it was precisely the opposite historical mode of thought and approach which was then particularly developed, and that it was not the ideas in history that were pursued but only a sense that was developed for the external world of facts. Attention was also drawn to the fact that, with regard to this last question, one can only come to clarity through spiritual science, because spiritual science alone can uncover the real driving forces of the historical evolution of humanity.

A spiritual science of this kind was not yet accessible to Humboldt. He spoke of ideas, but ideas indeed have no driving force [of their own]. Ideas as such are abstractions, as I mentioned here yesterday.[3] And anyone who might wish to find ideas as the driving forces of history would never be able to prove that ideas really do anything because they are nothing of real substantiality, and only something of substantiality can do something. Spiritual science points to real spiritual forces that are behind the sensible-physical facts, and it is in real spiritual forces such as these that the propelling forces of history lie, even though these spiritual forces will have to be expressed for human beings through ideas.

But we come to clarity concerning these things only when, from a spiritual-scientific standpoint, we look more deeply into the historical development of humanity and we will do so today in such a way that, through our considerations, certain facts come to us which, precisely for a discerning judgement of the situation of modern humanity, will prove to be of importance.

I have often mentioned[4] that spiritual science, if it looks at history, would actually have to pursue a symptomatology; a symptomatology constituted from the fact that one is aware that behind what takes it course as the stream of physical-sensible facts lie the driving spiritual forces. But everywhere in historical development there are times when what has real being and essence (*das eigentlich Wesenhafte*) comes as a symptom to the surface and can be judged discerningly from the phenomena only if one has the possibility to penetrate more deeply from one's awareness of these phenomena into the depths of historical development.

I would like to clarify this by a simple diagram. Let us suppose that this is a flow of historical facts (see diagram). The driving forces lie, for ordinary observation, below the flow of these facts. And if the eye of the soul observes the flow in this way, then the real activity of the driving forces would lie beneath it (red). But there are significant points in this flow of facts. And these significant points are distinguished by the fact that what is otherwise hidden comes here to the surface. Thus we can say: Here, in a particular phenomenon, which must only be properly evaluated, it was possible to become aware of something which otherwise is at work everywhere, but which does not show itself in such a significant manifestation.

Let us assume that this (see diagram) took place in some year of world history, let us say around 800 AD. What was significant

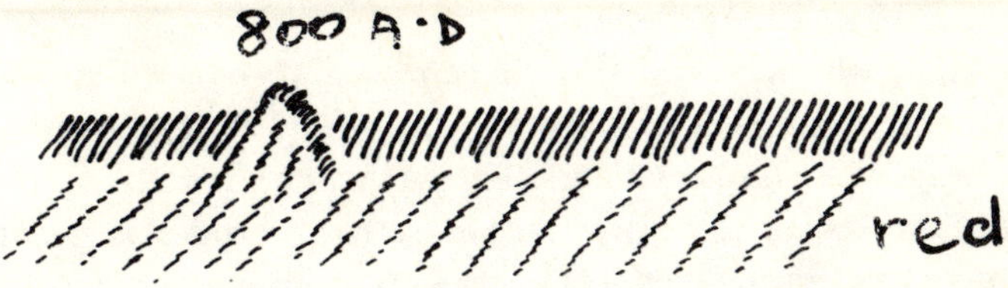

[handwritten annotation: 800 A.D, with hatched drawing labeled "red"]

for Europe, let us say for Western Europe, was of course at work before this and worked on afterwards, but it did not manifest itself in such a significant way in the time before and after as it did here. If one points to a way of looking at history like this, a way which looks to significant moments, such a method would be in complete accord with Goetheanism. For Goethe wished in general that all perception of the world should be directed to significant points and then, from what could be seen from such points, the remaining content of world events be recognized. Goethe says of this[5] that, within the abundance of facts, the important thing is to find a significant point from which the neighbouring areas can be viewed and from which much can be deciphered.

So let us take this year 800 AD. We can point here to a fact in the history of Western European humanity which, from the point of view of the usual approach to history, might seem insignificant – which one would perhaps not find worthy of attention for what is usually called history – but which, nevertheless, for a deeper view of humanity's development, is indeed significant. Around this year there was a kind of learned theological argument between the man who was a sort of court philosopher of the Frankish realm, Alcuin[6], and a Greek also living at that time in the kingdom of the Franks. The Greek, who was naturally at home in the particular soul-constitution of the Greek peoples which he had inherited, had wanted to reach a discerning judgement of the principles of Christianity and had come to the concept of redemption. He put the question: To whom, in the redemption through Christ Jesus, was the ransom actually paid? He, the Greek thinker, came to the solution that the ransom had been paid to Death. Thus, in a certain sense, it was a sort of redemption theory that this Greek developed from his thoroughly Greek mode of thinking, which was now just becoming acquainted with Christianity. The ransom was paid to Death by the cosmic powers.

Alcuin, who stood at that time in that theological stream which then became the determining one for the development of the Roman Catholic Church of the West, debated in the following way about what the Greek had argued. He said: Ransom can only be paid to a being who really exists. But death has no reality, death is only the outer limit of reality, death itself is not real and, therefore, the ransom money could not have been paid to Death.

Now criticism of Alcuin's way of thinking is not what matters here. For to someone who, to a certain extent, can see through the interrelations of the facts, the view that death is not something real resembles the view which says: Cold is not something real, it is just a decrease in warmth, it is only a lesser warmth. Because the cold isn't real I won't wear a winter coat in winter because I'm not going to protect myself against something that isn't real. But we will leave that aside. We want rather to take the argument between Alcuin and the Greek purely positively and will ask what was really happening there. For it is indeed quite noticeable that it is not the concept of redemption itself that is discussed. It is not discussed in such a way that in a certain sense both personalities, the Greek and the Roman Catholic theologian, accept the same point of view, but in such a way that the Roman Catholic theologian shifts the standpoint entirely before he takes it up at all. He does not go on speaking in the way he had just done, but moves the whole problem into a completely different direction. He asks: Is death something real or not? — and objects that, indeed, death is not real.

This directs us at the outset to the fact that two views are clashing here which arise out of completely different constitutions of soul. And, indeed, this is the case. The Greek continued, as it were, the direction which, in the Greek culture, had basically faded away between Plato and Aristotle. In Plato there was still something alive of the ancient wisdom of humanity; that wisdom which takes us across to the ancient Orient where, indeed, in ancient times a primal wisdom had lived — but which had then fallen more and more into decadence. In Plato, if we are able to understand him properly, we find the last offshoots, if I can so call them, of this primal oriental wisdom. And then, like a rapidly developing metamorphosis, Aristotelianism sets in which, fundamentally, presents a completely different constitution of soul from the Platonic one. Aristotelianism represents a completely different element in the development of humanity from Platonism. And, if we follow Aristotelianism further, it, too, takes on different forms, different metamorphoses, but all of which have a recognizable similarity. Thus we see how Platonism lives on like an ancient heritage in this Greek who has to contend against Alcuin, and how in Alcuin, on the other hand, Aristotelianism is already present. And we are directed, by looking at these two individuals, to that fluctuation which took place on European soil between two – one cannot really say world-views – but two human constitutions of soul, one of which has its origin in ancient times in the Orient, and another, which we do not find in the Orient but which, entering in later, arose in the central regions of civilization and was first grasped by Aristotle. In Aristotle, however, this only sounds a first quiet note, for much of Greek culture was still alive in him. It develops then with particular vehemence in the Roman culture within which it had been prepared long before Aristotle, and, indeed, before Plato. So that we see how, since the eighth century BC on the Italian peninsula a particular culture, or the first hints of it, was being prepared alongside that which lived on the Greek peninsula as a sort of last offshoot of the oriental constitution of soul. And when we go into the differences between these two modes of human thought we find important historical impulses. For what is expressed in these ways of thinking went over later into the feeling life of human beings; into the configuration of human actions and so on.

Now we can ask ourselves: So what was living in that which developed in ancient times as a world-view in the Orient, and which then, like a latecomer, found its [last] offshoots in Platonism – and, indeed, still in Neoplatonism? It was a highly spiritual culture which arose from an inner perception living pre-eminently in pictures, in imaginations; but pictures not permeated by full consciousness, not yet permeated by the full I-consciousness of human beings. In the spiritual life of the ancient Orient, of which the Veda and Vedanta are the last echoes, stupendous pictures opened up of what lives in the human being as the spiritual. But it existed in a – I beg you not to misunderstand the word and not to confuse it with usual dreaming – it existed in a dreamlike, dim way, so that this soul-life was not permeated (*durchwellt*) and irradiated (*durchstrahlt*) by what lives in the human being when he becomes clearly conscious of his 'I' and his own being. The oriental was well aware that his being existed before birth, that it returns through death to the spiritual world in which it existed before birth or conception. The oriental gazed on that which passed through births and deaths. But he did not see as such that inner feeling which lives in the 'I am'. It was as if it were dull and hazy, as though poured out in a broad perception of the soul (*Gesamtseelenanschauung*) which did not concentrate to such a point as that of the I-experience. Into what, then, did the oriental actually gaze when he possessed his instinctive perception?

One can still feel how this oriental soul-constitution was completely different from that of later humanity when, for an understanding of this and perhaps prepared through spiritual science, one sinks meditatively into those remarkable writings which are ascribed to Dionysius the Areopagite.[7] I will not go into the question of the authorship now, I have already spoken about it on a number of occasions. 'Nothingness' (*das Nichts*) is still spoken of there as a reality, and the existence of the external world, in the way one views it in ordinary consciousness, is simply contrasted against this [nothingness] as a different reality. This talk of nothingness then continues. In Scotus Erigena,[8] who lived at the court of Charles the Bald, one still finds echoes of it, and we find the last echo then in the fifteenth century in Nicolas of Cusa.[9] But what was meant by the nothingness one finds in Dionysius the Areopagite and of that which the oriental spoke of as something self-evident to him? This fades then completely. What was this nothingness for the oriental? It was something real for him. He turned his gaze to the world of the senses around him, and said: This sense-world is spread out in space, flows in time, and in ordinary life one says that what is extended in space and flows in time is *something*.

But what the oriental saw – that which was a reality for him, which passes through births and deaths – was not contained in the space in which the minerals are to be found, in which the plants unfold, the animals move and the human being as a physical being moves and acts. And it was also not contained in that time in which our thoughts, feelings and will-impulses occur. The oriental was fully aware that one must go beyond this space in which physical things are extended and move, and beyond this time in which our soul-forces of ordinary life are active. One must enter a completely different world; that world which, for the external existence of time and space, is a nothing but which, nevertheless, is something real. The oriental sensed something in contrast to the phenomena of the world which the European still senses at most in the realm of real numbers.

When a European has fifty francs he has something. If he spends twenty-five francs of this he still has twenty-five francs; if he then spends fifteen francs he still has ten; if he spends this he has nothing. If now he continues to spend he has five, ten, fifteen, twenty-five francs in debts. He still has nothing; but, indeed, he has something very real when, instead of simply an empty wallet, he has twenty-five or fifty francs in debts. In the real world it also signifies something very real if one has debts. There is a great difference in one's whole situation in life between having nothing and having fifty francs' worth of debts. These debts of fifty francs are forces just as influential on one's situation in life as, on the other side and in an opposite sense, are fifty francs of credit. In this area the European will probably admit to the reality of debts for, in the real world, there always has to be something there when one has debts. The debts that one has oneself may still seem a very negative amount, but for the person to whom they are owed they are a very positive amount!

So, when it is not just a matter of the individual but of the world, the opposite side of zero from the credit side is truly something very real. The oriental felt – not because he somehow speculated about it but because his perception necessitated it – he felt: Here, on the one side, I experience that which cannot be observed in space or in time; something which, for the things and events of space and time, is nothing but which, nevertheless, is a reality – but a different reality.

It was only through misunderstanding that there then arose what occidental civilization gave itself up to under the leadership of Rome – the creation of the world out of nothing with 'nothing' seen as absolute 'zero'. In the Orient, where these things were originally conceived, the world does not arise out of nothing but out of the reality I have just indicated. And an echo of what vibrates through all the oriental way of thinking right down to Plato – the impulse of eternity of an ancient world-view – lived in the Greek who, at the court of Charlemagne, had to debate with Alcuin. And in this theologian Alcuin there lived a rejection of the spiritual life for which, in the Orient, this 'nothing' was the outer form. And thus, when the Greek spoke of death, whose causes lie in the spiritual world, as something real, Alcuin could only answer: But death is nothing and therefore cannot receive ransom.

You see, the whole polarity between the ancient oriental way of thinking, reaching to Plato, and what followed later is expressed in this [one] significant moment when Alcuin debated at the court of Charlemagne with the Greek. For, what was it that had meanwhile entered into European civilization since Plato, particularly through the spread of Romanism? There had entered that way of thinking which one has to comprehend through the fact that it is directed primarily to what the human being experiences between birth and death. And the constitution of soul which occupies itself primarily with the human being's experiences between birth and death is the logical, legal one – the logical-dialectical-legal one. The Orient had nothing of a logical, dialectical nature and, least of all, a legal one. The Occident brought logical, legal thinking so strongly into the oriental way of thinking that we ourselves find religious feeling permeated with a legalistic element. In the Sistine Chapel in Rome, painted by the master-hand of Michelangelo, we see, looming towards us, Christ as Judge giving judgment on the good and the evil.

A legal, dialectical element has entered into the thoughts concerning the course of the world. This was completely alien to the oriental way of thinking. There was nothing there like guilt and atonement or redemption. For [in this oriental way of thinking] was precisely that view of the metamorphosis through which the eternal element [in the human being] transforms itself through births and deaths. There was that which lives in the concept of karma. Later, however, everything was fixed into a way of looking at things which is actually only valid for, and can only encompass, life between birth and death. But this life between birth and death was just what had evaded the oriental. He looked far more to the core of man's being. He had little understanding for what took place between birth and death. And now, within this occidental culture, the way of thinking which comprehends primarily what takes place within the span between birth and death increased [and did so] through those forces possessed by the human being by virtue of having clothed his soul-and-spirit nature with a physical and etheric body. In this constitution, in the inner experience of the soul-and-spirit element and in the nature of this experience, which arises through the fact that one is submerged with one's soul-and-spirit nature in a physical body, comes the inner comprehension of the 'I'. This is why it happens in the Occident that the human being feels an inner urge to lay hold of his 'I' as something divine. We see this urge, to comprehend the 'I' as something divine, arise in the medieval mystics; in Eckhart, in Tauler and in others. The comprehension of the 'I' crystallizes out with full force in the Middle (or Central) culture. Thus we can distinguish between the Eastern culture – the time in which the 'I' is first experienced, but dimly – and the Middle (or Central) culture – primarily that in which the 'I' is experienced. And we see how this 'I' is experienced in the most manifold metamorphoses. First of all in that dim, dawning way in which it arises in Eckhart, Tauler and other mystics, and then more and more distinctly during the development of all that can originate out of this I-culture.

We then see how, within the I-culture of the Centre, another aspect arises. At then end of the eighteenth century something comes to the fore in Kant[10] which, fundamentally, cannot be explained out of the onward flow of this I-culture. For what is it that arises through Kant? Kant looks at our perception, our apprehension (*Erkennen*), of nature and cannot come to terms with it. Knowledge of nature, for him, breaks down into subjective views (*Subjektivitäten*); he does not penetrate as far as the 'I' despite the fact that he continually speaks of it and even, in some categories, in his perceptions of time and space, would like to encompass all nature through the 'I'. Yet he does not push through to a true experience of the 'I'. He also constructs a practical philosophy with the categorical imperative which is supposed to manifest itself out of unfathomable regions of the human soul. Here again the 'I' does not appear.

In Kant's philosophy it is strange. The full weight of dialectics, of logical-dialectical-legal thinking is there, in which everything is tending towards the 'I', but he cannot reach the point of really understanding the 'I' philosophically. There must be something preventing him here. Then comes Fichte, a pupil of Kant's, who with full force wishes his whole philosophy to well up out of the 'I' and who, through its simplicity, presents as the highest tenet of his philosophy the sentence: 'I am'. And everything that is truly scientific must follow from this 'I am'. One should be able, as it were, to deduce, to read from this 'I am' an entire picture of the world. Kant cannot reach the 'I am'. Fichte immediately afterwards, while still a pupil of Kant's, hurls the 'I am' at him. And everyone is amazed – this is a pupil of Kant's speaking like this! And Fichte says:[11] As far as he can understand it, Kant, if he could really think to the end, would have to think the same as me. It is so inexplicable to Fichte that Kant thinks differently from him, that he says: If Kant would only take things to their full conclusion, he would have to think [as I do]; he, too, would have to come to the 'I am'. And Fichte expresses this even more clearly by saying: I would rather take the whole of Kant's critique for a random game of ideas haphazardly thrown together than to consider it the work of a human mind, if my philosophy did not logically follow from Kant's. Kant, of course, rejects this. He wants nothing to do with the conclusions drawn by Fichte.

We now see how there follows on from Fichte what then flowered as German idealistic philosophy in Schelling and Hegel, and which provoked all the battles of which I spoke, in part, in my lectures on the limits to a knowledge of nature.[12] But we find something curious. We see how Hegel lives in a crystal-clear [mental] framework of the logical-dialectical-legal element and draws from it a world-view – but a world-view that is interested only in what occurs between birth and death. You can go through the whole of Hegel's philosophy and you will find nothing that goes beyond birth and death. It confines everything in world history, religion, art and science solely to experiences occurring between birth and death.

What then is the strange thing that happened here? Now, what came out in Fichte, Schelling and Hegel – this strongest development of the Central culture in which the 'I' came to full consciousness, to an inner experience – was still only a reaction, a last reaction to something else. For one can understand Kant only when one bears the following properly in mind. (I am coming now to yet another significant point to which a great deal can be traced). You see, Kant was still – this is clearly evident from his earlier writings – a pupil of the rationalism of the eighteenth century, which lived with genius in Leibnitz and pedantically in Wolff. One can see that for this rationalism the important thing was not to come truly to a spiritual reality. Kant therefore rejected it – this 'thing in itself' as he called it – but the important thing for him was to prove. Sure proof! Kant's writings are remarkable also in this respect. He wrote his *Critique of Pure Reason* in which he is actually asking: 'How must the world be so that things can be proved in it?' Not 'What are the realities in it?' But he actually asks: 'How must I imagine the world so that logically, dialectically, I can give proofs in it?' This is the only point he is concerned with and thus he tries in his *Prologomena* to give every future metaphysics which has a claim to being truly scientific, a metaphysics for what in his way of thinking can be proven: 'Away with everything else! The devil take the reality of the world – just let me have the art of proving! What's it to me what reality is; if I can't prove it I shan't trouble myself over it!'

Those individuals did not, of course, think in this way who wrote books like, for example, Christian Wolff's[13] *Vernünftige Gedanken von Gott, der Welt und der Seele des Menschen, auch allen Dingen überhaupt* (*Reasoned Thoughts on God, the World, and the Soul of Man, and All Things Generally*). What mattered for them was to have a clean, self-contained system of proof, in the way that they see proof. Kant lived in this sphere, but there was still something there which, although an excrescence squeezed out of the world-view of the Centre, nevertheless fitted into it. But Kant had something else which makes it inexplicable how he could become Fichte's teacher. And yet he gives Fichte a stimulus, and Fichte comes back at him with the strong emphasis of the 'I am'; comes back, indeed, not with proofs – one would not look for these in Fichte – but with a fully developed inner life of soul. In Fichte there emerges, with all the force of the inner life of soul, that which, in the Wolffians and Leibnitzites, can seem insipid. Fichte constructs his philosophy, in a wealth of pure concepts, out of the 'I am'; but in *him* they are filled with life. So, too, are they in Schelling and in Hegel. So what then had happened with Kant who was the bridge? Now, one comes to the significant point when one traces how Kant developed. Something else became of this pupil of Wolff by virtue of the fact that the English philosopher, David Hume,[14] awoke him, as Kant himself says, out of his dull dogmatic slumber. What is it that entered Kant here, which Fichte could no longer understand? There entered into Kant here – it fitted badly in his case because he was too involved with the culture of Central Europe – that which is now the culture of the West. This came to meet him in the person of David Hume and it was here that the culture of the West entered Kant. And in what does the peculiarity [of this culture] lie? In the oriental culture we find that the 'I' still lives below, dimly, in a dream-like state in the soul-experiences which express themselves, spread out, in imaginative pictures. In the Western culture we find that, in a certain sense, the 'I' is smothered (*erdrückt*) by the purely external phenomena (*Tatsachen*). The 'I' is indeed present, and is present not dimly, but bores itself into the phenomena. And here, for example, people develop a strange psychology. They do not talk here about the soul-life in the way Fichte did, who wanted to work out everything from the one point of the 'I', but they talk about thoughts which come together by association. People talk about feelings, mental pictures and sensations, and say these associate – and also will-impulses associate. One talks about the inner soul-life in terms of thoughts which associate.

Fichte speaks of the 'I'; this radiates out thoughts. In the West the 'I' is completely omitted because it is absorbed – soaked up by the thoughts and feelings which one treats as though they were independent of it, associating and separating again. And one follows the life of the soul as though mental pictures linked up and separated. Read Spencer,[15] read John Stuart Mill,[16] read the American philosophers. When they come to talk of psychology there is this curious view that does not exclude the 'I' as in the Orient, because it is developed dimly there, but which makes full demand of the 'I'; letting it, however, sink down into the thinking, feeling and willing life of the soul. One could say: In the oriental the 'I' is still *above* thinking, feeling and willing; it has not yet descended to the level of thinking, feeling and willing. In the human being of the Western culture the 'I' is already *below* this sphere. It is below the surface of thinking, feeling and willing so that it is no longer noticed, and thinking, feeling and willing are then spoken of as independent forces.

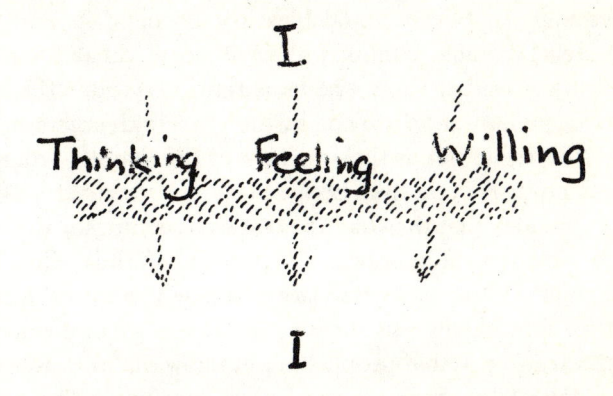

I.

Thinking   Feeling   Willing

I

This is what came to Kant in the form of the philosophy of David Hume. Then the Central region of the earth's culture still set itself against this with all force in Fichte, Schelling, and Hegel. After them the culture of the West overwhelms everything that is there, with Darwinism and Spencerism.

One will only be able to come to an understanding of what is living in humanity's development if one investigates these deeper forces. One then finds that something developed in a natural way in the Orient which actually was purely a spiritual life. In the Central areas something developed which was dialectical-legal, which actually brought forth the idea of the State, because it is to this that it can be applied. It is such thinkers as Fichte, Schelling and Hegel who, with enormous sympathy, construct a unified image (*Gebilde*) of the State. But then a culture emerges in the West which proceeds from a constitution of soul in which the 'I' is absorbed, takes its course below the level of thinking, feeling and willing; and where, in the mental and feeling life, people speak of associations. If only one would apply this thinking to the economic life! That is its proper place. People went completely amiss when they started applying [this thinking] to something other than the economic life. *There* it is great, is of genius. And had Spencer, John Stuart Mill and David Hume applied to the institutions of the economic life what they wasted on philosophy it would have been magnificent. If the human beings living in Central Europe had limited to the State what is given them as their natural endowment, and if they had not, at the same time, also wanted thereby to include the spiritual life and the economic life, something magnificent could have come out of it. For, with what Hegel was able to think, with what Fichte was able to think, one would have been able – had one remained within the legal-political configuration which, in the threefold organism, we wish to separate out as the structure of the State[17] – to attain something truly great. But, because there hovered before these minds the idea that they had to create a structure for the State which included the economic life and the spiritual life, there arose only caricatures in the place of a true form for the State. And the spiritual life was anyway only a heritage of the ancient Orient. It was just that people did not know that they were still living from this heritage of the ancient East. The useful statements, for example, of Christian theology – indeed, the useful statements still within our materialistic sciences – are either the heritage of the ancient East, or a changeling of dialectical-legal thinking, or are already adopted, as was done by Spencer and Mill, from the Western culture which is particularly suited for the economic life.

Thus the spiritual thinking of the ancient Orient had been distributed over the earth, but in an instinctive way that is no longer of any use today. Because today it is decadent, it is dialectical-political thinking which was rendered obsolete by the world catastrophe [World War I]. For there was no one less suited to thinking economically than the pupils of Fichte, Schelling and Hegel. When they began to create a State which, above all, was to become great through its economy, they had of necessity (*selbstverständlich*) to fail, for this was not what, by nature, was endowed to them. In accordance with the historical development of humanity, spiritual thinking, political thinking and economic thinking were apportioned to the East, the Centre, and the West respectively. But we have arrived at a point of humanity's development when understanding, a common understanding, must spread equally over all humanity. How can this come about?

This can only happen out of the initiation-culture, out of the new spiritual science, which does not develop one-sidedly, but considers everything that appears in all areas as a threefoldness that has evolved of its own accord. This science must really consider the threefold aspect also in social life; in this case (as a threefoldness) encompassing the whole earth. Spiritual science, however, cannot be extended through natural abilities; it can only be spread by people accepting those who see into these things, who can really experience the spiritual sphere, the political sphere and the economic sphere as three separate areas. The unity of human beings all over the earth is due to the fact that they combine in themselves what was divided between three spheres. They themselves organize it in the social organism in such a way that it can exist in harmony before their eyes. This, however, can only follow from spiritual-scientific training. And we stand here at a point where we must say: In ancient times we see individual personalities, we see them expressing in their words what was the spirit of the time. But when we examine it closely – in the oriental culture, for example – we find that, fundamentally, there lives instinctively in the masses a constitution of soul which in a remarkable, quite natural way was in accord with what these individuals spoke.

This correspondence, however, became less and less. In our times we see the development of the opposite extreme. We see instincts arising in the masses which are the opposite of what is beneficial for humanity. We see things arising that absolutely call for the qualities that may arise in individuals who are able to penetrate the depths of spiritual science. No good will come from instincts, but only from the understanding (that Dr Unger also spoke of here[18]) which, as is often stressed, every human being can bring towards the spiritual investigator if he really opens himself to healthy human reason. Thus there will come a culture in which the single individual, with his ever-deeper penetration into the depths of the spiritual world, will be of particular importance, and in which the one who penetrates in this way will be valued, just as someone who works in some craft is valued. One does not go to the tailor to have boots made or to the shoemaker to be shaved, so why should people go to someone else for what one needs as a world-view other than to the person who is initiated into it? And it is, indeed, just this that, particularly today and in the most intense sense, is necessary for the good of human beings even though there is a reaction against it, which shows how humanity still resists what is beneficial for it. This is the terrible battle – the grave situation – in which we find ourselves.

At no other time has there been a greater need to listen carefully to what individuals know concerning one thing or another. Nor has there been a greater need for people with knowledge of specific subject areas to be active in social life – not from a belief in authority but out of common sense and out of agreement based on common sense. But, to begin with, the instincts oppose this and people believe that some sort of good can be achieved from levelling everything. This is the serious battle in which we stand. Sympathy and antipathy are of no help here, nor is living in slogans. Only a clear observation of the facts can help. For today great questions are being decided – the questions as to whether the individual or the masses have significance. In other times this was not important because the masses and the individual were in accord with one another; individuals were, in a certain sense, simply speaking for the masses. We are approaching more and more that time when the individual must find completely within himself the source of what he has to find and which he has then to put into the social life; and [what we are now seeing] is only the last resistance against this validity of the individual and an ever larger and larger number of individuals. One can see plainly how that which spiritual science shows is also proved everywhere in these significant points. We talk of associations which are necessary in the economic life, and use a particular thinking for this. This has developed in the culture of the West from letting thoughts associate. If one could take what John Stuart Mill does with logic, if one could remove those thoughts from that sphere and apply them to the economic life, they would fit there. The associations which would then come in there would be exactly those which do not fit into psychology. Even in what appears in the area of human development, spiritual science follows reality.

Thus spiritual science, if fully aware of the seriousness of the present world situation, knows what a great battle is taking place between the threefold social impulse that can come from spiritual science and that which throws itself against this threefoldness as the wave of Bolshevism, which would lead to great harm (*Unheil*) amongst humanity. And there is no third element other than these two. The battle has to take place between these two. People must see this! Everything else is already decadent. Whoever looks with an open mind at the conditions in which we are placed, must conclude that it is essential today to gather all our forces together so that this whole terrible Ahrimanic affair can be repulsed.

This building stands here,[19] incomplete though it is for the time being. Today we cannot get from the Central countries that which for the most part, and in addition to what has come to us from the neutral states, has brought this building to this stage. We must have contributions from the countries of the former Entente. Understanding must be developed here for what is to become a unified culture containing spirit, politics and economics. For people must get away from a one-sided tendency and must follow those who also understand something of politics and economics, who do not work only in dialectics, but, also being engaged with economic impulses, have insight into the spiritual, and do not want to create states in which the State itself can run the economy. The Western peoples will have to realize that something else must evolve in addition to the special gift they will have in the future with regard to forming economic associations. The skill in forming associations has so far been applied at the wrong end, i.e. in the field of psychology. What must evolve is understanding of the political-state element, which has other sources than the economic life, and also of the spiritual element. But at present the Central countries lie powerless, so people in the Western regions – one could not expect this of the Orient – will have to see what the purpose of this building is! It is necessary for us to consider what must be done so that real provision is made for a new culture that should be presented everywhere in the university education of the future – here we have to show the way. In the foundation of the Waldorf Schools the culture has proved to be capable of bringing light into primary education. But for this we need the understanding support of the widest circles.

Above all we need the means. For everything which, in a higher or lower sense, is called a school, we need the frame of mind I have already tried to awaken at the opening of the Waldorf School in Stuttgart.[20] I said in my opening speech there: 'This is *one* Waldorf school. It is well and good that we have it, but for itself it is nothing; it is only something if, in the next quarter of a year, we build ten such Waldorf schools and then others'. The world did not understand this, it had no money for such a thing. For it rests on the standpoint: Oh, the ideals are too lofty, too pure for us to bring dirty money to them; better to keep it in our pockets; that's the proper place for dirty money. The ideals, oh, they're too pure, one can't contaminate them with money! Of course, with purity of this kind the embodiment of ideals cannot be attained, if dirty money is not brought to them. And thus we have to consider that, up to now, we have stopped at one Waldorf school which cannot progress properly because in the autumn we found ourselves in great money difficulties. These have been obviated for the time being, but at Easter we shall be faced with them again. And then, after a comparatively short time, we will ask: Should we give up? And we shall have to give up if, before then, an understanding is not forthcoming which dips vigorously into its pockets.

It is thus a matter of awakening understanding in this respect. I don't believe that much understanding would arise if we were to say that we wanted something for the building in Dornach, or some such thing – as has been shown already. But – and one still finds understanding for this today – if one wants to create sanatoria or the like, one gets money, and as much as one wants! This is not exactly what we want – we don't want to build a host of sanatoria – we agree fully with creating them as far as they are necessary; but here it is a matter, above all, of nurturing that spiritual culture whose necessity will indeed prove itself through what this course[21] has attempted to accomplish. This is what I tried to suggest, to give a stimulus to what I expressed here a few days ago, in the words 'World Fellowship of Schools' (*Weltschulverein*).[22]

Our German friends have departed but it is not a question of depending on them for this 'World Fellowship'. It depends on those who, as friends, have come here, for the most part from all possible regions of the non-German world – and who are still sitting here now – that they understand these words 'World Fellowship of Schools' because it is vital that we found school upon school in all areas of the world out of the pedagogical spirit which rules in the Waldorf School. We have to be able to extend this school until we are able to move into higher education of the kind we are hoping for here. For this, however, we have to be in a position to complete this building and everything that belongs to it, and be constantly able to support that which is necessary in order to work here; to be productive, to work on the further extension of all the separate sciences in the spirit of spiritual science.

People ask one how much money one needs for all this. One cannot say how much, because there never is an uppermost limit. And, of course, we will not be able to found a World Fellowship of Schools simply by creating a committee of twelve or fifteen or thirty people who work out nice statutes as to how a World Fellowship of Schools of this kind should work. That is all pointless. I attach no value to programmes or to statutes but only to the work of active people who work with understanding. It will be possible to establish this World Fellowship – well, we shall not be able to go to London for some time -- in the Hague or some such place, if a basis can be created, and by other means if the friends who are about to go to Norway or Sweden or Holland, or any other country – England, France, America and so on – awaken in every human being whom they can reach the well-founded conviction that there *has* to be a World Fellowship of Schools. It ought to go through the world like wildfire that a World Fellowship must arise to provide the material means for the spiritual culture that is intended here.

If one is able in other matters, as a single individual, to convince possibly hundreds and hundreds of people, why should one not be able in a short time – for the decline is happening so quickly that we only have a short time – to have an effect on many people as a single individual, so that if one came to the Hague a few weeks later one would see how widespread was the thought that: 'The creation of a World Fellowship of Schools is necessary, it is just that there are no means for it.' What we are trying to do from Dornach is an historical necessity. One will only be able to talk of the inauguration of this

World Fellowship of Schools when the idea of it already exists. It is simply utopian to set up committees and found a World Fellowship – this is pointless! But to work from person to person, and to spread quickly the realization, the well-founded realization, that it is so necessary – this is what must precede the founding. Spiritual science lives in realities. This is why it does not get involved with proposals of schemes for a founding but points to what has to happen in reality – and human beings are indeed realities – so that such a thing has some prospects.

So what is important here is that we finally learn from spiritual science how to stand in real life. I would never get involved with a simply utopian founding of the World Fellowship of Schools, but would always be of the opinion that this World Fellowship can only come about when a sufficiently large number of people are convinced of its necessity. It must be created so that what is necessary for humanity – it has already proved to be so from our course here – can happen. This World Fellowship of Schools must be created.

Please see what is meant by this Fellowship in all international life, in the right sense! I would like, in this request, to round off today what, in a very different way in our course, has spoken to humanity through those who were here and of whom we have the hope and the wish that they carry it out into the world. The World Fellowship of Schools can be the answer of the world to what was put before it like a question; a question taken from the real forces of human evolution, that is, human history. So let what can happen for the World Fellowship of Schools, in accordance with the conviction you have been able to gain here, happen! In this there rings out what I wanted to say today.

Dornach, 22 October 1920

The fifteenth century ushered in an era for the civilized humanity of the Northern Hemisphere, in which the human individuality began to develop more and more in full I-consciousness. The forces which elaborate this I-consciousness will grow increasingly stronger and all the phenomena of life – of life in the broadest sense – will take place in the sign of this development of the individuality. This, however, means that what comes from the spiritual world and plays into our physical world will take such a course that, in humanity as a whole, the individual element of the human being will take on greater importance. For it is not simply a matter of individual human beings thinking in an egotistical way, 'we are individuals': it is rather a matter of the whole development of humanity taking such a course that the individual human element can work into it.

Every age, every epoch, that we can trace in the course of human evolution developed some particular quality, just as now it is that of individuality. These characteristics are impressed into human evolution through the particular action of spiritual powers working into the physical life of humanity on earth. But precisely because of the separateness that we see in the individual human being today when the individuality is developing – when I-consciousness is developing fully, when the consciousness-soul is, as it were, giving itself contour, becoming integrated in itself – the special characteristics of this epoch are not directed from the spiritual world as they were in earlier epochs, and very exceptional things are making their appearance within humanity's evolution. And the human being who, through the development of his individuality is being increasingly educated for freedom, must also take up a conscious stand more and more to what results from this. Above all it is essential that a social life take shape, but a social life which, from our point of view, must have deep inner foundations. This must take shape despite the fact that the strong egoistical forces of the consciousness-soul, which are opposed to a social life, are emerging ever more strongly from the depths of existence. On the one side we have the strong egoistical forces of the consciousness-soul and, on the other, the all-the-greater necessity of founding a social life consciously. And we must take a conscious stand towards everything that can foster this social living together. We have shown in the past,[1] and from the most varied points of view, how differently the human beings of the West, the European Centre, and of the East are placed in the whole course of human evolution. We have pointed to different things that are peculiar to the human beings of the East, Central Europe and the West. And we want now to turn to a phenomenon that can already show us externally how these differences within humanity express themselves in the civilized world.

We know that, under the influence of our modern scientific way of thinking about social life, a certain view of life has been developed. This comes to expression particularly strongly in the broad masses of the proletariat which has come into being in our technological age, our intellectual age. I have presented all this, insofar as it touches the social question, in the first part of my *Towards Social Renewal* (*Kernpunkt der sociale Frage*). Today I want only to indicate the diversity of views among the broad masses of humanity concerning the social question. We have, clearly differentiated, the social views of, let us say, the proletariat, which then, however, colour other strata of the population. We have, distinct from that of other peoples, the conception of life held in the West, especially in the Anglo-Saxon countries. In these countries, under the influence of the modern technology and industry, there has also developed among the broad masses that materialistic concept of life which has often been characterized here. This arose side by side with materialism or was directly produced through the materialism of other classes. This socialist conception of life, however, developed in such a way that it stands entirely under the aegis of economic strife, for it is permeated by economic concepts, thoughts and struggles that are little penetrated by the struggle for a philosophy of life (*Lebensanschauungskämpfen*). This is the characteristic stamp of what is going on in the socialist world of the Anglo-Saxon West. And because the actual character of modern public life as a whole has hitherto been the economic life, it was from the economic conditions of the Anglo-Saxon proletariat that the impulses of socialism arose.

The impulses coming to expression in the Great Strike movement are significant precisely as a characteristic of what is taking shape in this respect in the West. Even if it seems that the discrepancies which are there could be settled, it only seems so, for such settlements would not be real; very significant effects will issue from the deeper forces playing in these conflicts. And although, by virtue of the whole make-up of the West, no genuine philosophies or concepts of life (*Lebensauffassung*), develop from these impulses, we can nevertheless clearly perceive how the views of life which do develop, and which have developed in recent times, have taken their incentive from the impulses present there [in the West].

In fact, Karl Marx,[2] who was born in Central Europe and was nurtured in the Central European stream of thought, had to go to England in order to absorb the practical impulses (*Lebensimpulse*) which had developed there. He, however, transformed them into a theory, into a conception of life. And Marxism as a theory of life has found little external expression in the West. Where it *has* come to external expression, however, is in Central Europe. In the aims of the social democracy there, it has taken on fully the nature of a philosophy. What in the West are economic impulses leading to economic conflict, were diverted and fixed into legal-political concepts which lived then in Central Europe in the second half of the nineteenth century and on into the twentieth century as Marxist ideology and took hold of the broad masses of the population. It also found its way into the areas stretching towards the East, to those parts of Europe which begin to take on the character of the East. But here again it expressed itself in another form. Economic in the West; political in the Centre; and in the East it assumes a distinctly religious character. A distortion exists, which occurred with the inundation of the East through Peter the Great[3] – and now Lenin[4] and Trotsky.[5] This arises because the Bolshevism making itself felt there is in fact a foreign import. If it were not for that distinction it would be far more evident that, even now, Bolshevism has a strong religious element which, however, is completely materialistic. It works through earlier religious impulses and will continue to do so. And it is precisely in this that its terrible aspect will show itself throughout all Asia, because it works with all the fervour of a religious impulse. The social impulse in the West is economic, in Central Europe is political, and works with a religious fervour eastwards from Russia over into Asia. Over and against these impulses which move through the development of humanity there is a great deal that is utterly unimportant. And anyone who does not see, in the most intense sense, something of symptomatic importance in such things as the present [1920] strike of the British miners simply has no understanding at all of the foment of deeper forces in the whole of our present development.

All this, however, which can be described externally in this way, has deeper causes – causes which lie ultimately in the spiritual world. The more recent life of humanity can only be understood if one understands this differentiation – a differentiation into the Western economic element, the Central European political-legal one, and the religious element – the spiritual element in the East which takes on a religious character but is actually the momentum of a decadent spirituality that still finds expression in the East. This shows itself so strongly that one must say: It is natural for the West – and this is carried out thoroughly by it – to have everything of an economic nature; purely economic aspirations can have no success in the Centre because all economic aims there assume a political character. The great outer failure in Eastern Europe has come about because, through the tradition of Peter the Great, what arises out of a spiritual-religious impulse, i.e. Pan-slavism or Slavophilism, has taken on a political character. Behind this political character, which has produced all the dreadful things that have developed in the European East and has set its characteristic stamp on all the aspirations of the East since Peter the Great, there is, fundamentally, always the spiritual tendency of Byzantium, that is spiritual Byzantine religiosity, and so on. The individual phenomena of history become comprehensible only if they can be seen in this light. One can say: To a certain extent, everything that is still in Europe – also towards the West, even into France – can be reckoned as belonging to the European Centre, for what is characteristic of the West is actually Anglo-

Saxon. And, in its basic instincts, this 'Anglo-Saxondom' moves completely with the impulses that have arisen naturally within human development in the last three or four centuries. It was thus precisely in the West that these impulses could best bring about the development of all that was then for d upon the social life through the modern scientific way of thinking and all its achievements. This way of thinking and its achievements, together with the inherent nature of Anglo-Saxondom, was the foundation for the world dominion of the Anglo-Saxon. The brilliant rise of commerce, trade and industry which has come out of modern science, everything which led to the great colonizations, has arisen, in fact, through the confluence of the natural-scientific mode of thought and the character of Anglo-Saxondom. And this was sensed deep down in the instincts of the West.

One can actually point to a significant moment of modern historical development, to the year 1651, when the ingenious Cromwell with his Navigation Act[6] brought about that configuration in English navigation and in all English trade which was the foundation for everything in the West which later arose. One can also point to how, for outwardly inexplicable reasons, French merchant shipping suffered its greatest decline just as Napoleon's star was in the ascendant. What takes place in the West takes place out of the forces lying in the actual direction of humanity's development. It takes place out of a completely economic way of thinking, out of the impulses of economic ideas. This is why everything which comes from Central Europe and is conceived not out of economic points of view, but out of political-legal-militaristic ones must succumb to them. We have a crude example of how, based on a political-military standpoint, Napoleon, with his 'Continental System',[7] tried to counteract from the European continent everything that had resulted from Cromwell's Navigation Act. This Navigation Act was conceived and created entirely out of economic instincts. Napoleon's 'Continental System' at the beginning of the nineteenth century was a political conception. But a political conception is something that projects from earlier times into the modern age – it is antiquated, is actually an anachronism. This is why this political conception could be no match for the modern conception from which the Navigation Act arose. On the other hand, in the West where thinking follows the lines of economics in the sense of the new age, political affairs, even if they take an unfavourable course, do not fundamentally have any harmful effect.

Consider the fact that from Europe France colonized North America. She lost these colonies to England. The colonies freed themselves again. The first, the French colonization in the eighteenth century, was a political act and bore no fruit. The English colonization in North America was entirely out of economic impulses. The political element could be destroyed – North America freed itself and the political connection no longer existed. But the economic connections remained intact.

Thus are things linked in human evolution. And we can safely say that history also shows that when two do the same thing it is in fact not the same. When Cromwell, at the right time and out of economic impulses, created his Navigation Act – which, for the other powers, was extraordinarily tyrannical and even, one could say, brutal – this arose nevertheless from an economic thinking. When, in modern times, Tirpitz[8] created the German navy and merchant fleet it was conceived politically, purely politically and without any economic impulse – in fact, against all economic instincts. Today it has been wiped off the face of the earth because it was planned and conceived contrary to the course of human evolution. And thus it could be shown, with regard to all individual phenomena, how this, let us say historical threefoldness, really does exist; in the East, but in a decadent form today, something which points back to ancient times of Eastern evolution and has a spiritual character; in the Centre something which today is also antiquated and always, to a greater or lesser extent, takes on the form of the political-legal-militaristic; in the West the State is really only a decoration, the political has no real significance – what preponderates here is economic thinking. Whereas Germany has gone to pieces because the State has absorbed the economy, because industry and commerce have submerged and bowed down under the power of the State, we see in the West how the State is sucked up by the economic life and everything is flooded by the economic life. This, viewed externally, is the differentiation covering the modern civilized world.

But what one can view in this way externally is, after all,

basically brought to the visible surface only from the underlying depths of the spiritual world. Everything in the spiritual development of modern times is designed towards setting up the individuality — the individuality in the West in a Western way, in an economic way; the individuality of the Centre in the already antiquated political-militaristic way; the individuality of the East in an antiquated way, in accordance with the ancient spirituality that is now completely decadent. This has to be borne by the spiritual world, and it is borne by the fact that both in the West and the East — we shall consider only these two regions for the time being — a peculiar and deeply significant phenomenon is appearing. And it is this: very many people — at least relatively many — are being born who do not follow the regular course of reincarnation.

You see, this is why it is so difficult to speak about such a problem as reincarnation, because one cannot speak about it in the abstract sense that is so popular nowadays. For it is a problem pointing indeed to something that is a significant reality in the evolution of humanity, but it can have exceptions. And we see how both in the East and the West — we shall have to speak of the Centre in later lectures — people are born whom we cannot regard in such a way that we can say: There lives in this person, in the completely usual way, an individuality that was there in an earlier life, and then again in a subsequent earlier life, and which will be there in a later life and again in a still later life. Such reincarnations form the regular course of human evolution, but there are exceptions. What confronts us as a human being in human form does not always have to be as it outwardly appears. The outer appearance can, in fact, be just appearance. It is possible for us to confront human beings in human form who only appear to be human beings of the kind that are subject to repeated lives on earth. In reality these are human bodies with a physical, etheric and astral body — but there are other beings incarnated here, beings who use these people in order to work through them. There are in fact a large number of people, for example in the West, who are not simply reincarnated human beings but are the bearers of beings who have taken an extremely premature path of development and who should only appear in the form of humanity at a later stage of their evolution. Now these beings do not make use of the whole human organism but use chiefly the metabolic system of these Western human beings. Of the three members of the human nature they use the metabolic system and do so in such a way that, through these human beings, they work into the physical world. For one who can observe life with a certain accuracy, people of this kind even show outwardly that this is how it is with them. Thus, for example, a large number of those individuals who belong to Anglo-Saxon secret societies and who have great influence – we have spoken on a number of occasions in past years of the role of these secret societies[9] – are actually the bearers of premature existences of this kind which, through the metabolic system of certain people, work into the world and seek out a field of action through human bodies and do not live in normal regular incarnations. The leading personalities of certain sects are of this nature, and the overwhelming majority of a very widespread sect that has a great following in the West is made up of individuals of this kind. In this way a completely different spirituality is working into present-day human beings and it will be an essential task to be able to take up a stand towards life from this point of view.

One should not think in an abstract way that everywhere and without exception human beings are subject to repeated lives on earth. This would mean that we do not attribute to external semblance the quality of semblance. To face the truth means even in cases like these, to seek truth; to seek reality where outer appearance is so deceptive that beings other than human beings are incorporated in human form, in a part of the human being, namely in the metabolic system. But they also work in the trunk, in the rhythmic system and in the sensory-nervous system. There are in fact three kinds of beings of this nature who incarnate in this way through the metabolic system of different people of the West.

The first kind of beings are beings that have a particular attraction to what, in a sense, are the elemental forces of the earth; that have an inclination towards, a feeling for the elemental forces of the earth and are thus able to sense how, in any particular place, colonization could be carried out in accordance with the conditions of the climate and any other conditions of the earth, or how a trading connection can be established there, and so on.

The second kind of spirits of this nature are those that set themselves the task within their sphere of action of suppressing consciousness of self, of preventing full consciousness of the consciousness-soul from emerging, and thus produce in other people around them, amongst whom something like this spreads like an epidemic, a certain desire not to call themselves to account concerning the real motives behind their actions. One could say that such an utterly untrue report, or such an utterly untrue document, as the one by the Oxford professors that has been published in the last few days[10] – such an utterly, even absurdly, untruthful document – must be accounted to the pupilship of this untruthful element which does not wish to look into the real impulses, but glosses over them; uses beautiful words, and all the while there is beneath it nothing, basically, but untruthful impulses. I am not suggesting here that these Oxford professors – who are probably perfectly upright men in themselves (I do not impute strong Ahrimanic impulses to them) – are themselves bearers of such premature beings; but the pupilship to such beings lies within them. These [second kind of] beings, therefore, incarnate through the rhythmic system of certain people in the West.

The third kind of beings that work in the West are those which make it their task to cause the individual abilities in the human being to be forgotten – those abilities which we bring with us from the spiritual worlds when, through conception and birth, we come into physical existence – and to turn human beings more or less into a stereotyped replica of their nation. This is what this third kind of being gives itself as its special task: to prevent the human being from coming to individual spirituality.

So, while the first kind of beings had an affinity with the elemental nature of the ground of the earth, of the climate and so on, the second kind has a particular tendency to breed a certain superficial, untruthful element, and the third type of being the tendency to root out individual abilities and to turn people more or less into a stereotype, a copy of their nation, their race. This last class of beings incarnates in the West through the head system, through the sensory-nervous system. Thus we have here, observed from different angles, the characteristic of the Western world. We have characterized it, if

I may put it so, by getting to know a fairly large number of people who are scattered in secret societies, in sects and the like, but whose humanity is constituted in the fact that it is not simply a matter of repeated incarnations, but the incarnation, in a way, of beings who in their development are prematurely here on the earth and who, therefore, attract particular followers or radiate like an epidemic their own exceptional qualities onto other human beings. These three different types of being do indeed work through human beings and we understand human character only if we know what I have just related – if we know that what lives in public life cannot be simply explained superficially but has to be explained in terms of the intrusion of spiritual forces of this kind.

The appearance in Western human beings of these three kinds of forces, of beings at this particular stage of development, is encouraged by the fact that it is given to the West to develop a specifically economic way of thinking. The economic life is, as it were, the ground and soil from which something like this can spring up. And what then, in total, is the task these beings have set themselves?

They have set themselves the task of keeping life as a whole restricted to the mere life of economics. They seek gradually to root out everything else – everything of the spiritual life which even where it is most active, has shrunk into the abstractness of Puritanism – to root out spiritual life, to chip away the political life and to absorb everything into the life of economics. In the West the people who come into the world in this way are the real enemies and opponents of the threefold impulse. The beings of the first type prevent the emergence of an economic life that stands as an independent entity alongside the political-legal and spiritual facets of the social organism. The beings of the second type, who make superficiality, phrase-mongering and untruthfulness their task, seek to prevent the establishing, alongside the economic life, of an independent democratic life of the State. And the third kind of being – those that suppress the individual abilities of the human being and do not want the human being to be anything other than a kind of stereotype of his race, his nation – work against the emancipation and independence of the spiritual life.

Thus in the West there are such forces which work in this way against the impulse of the threefold social organism. And anyone who, in a deeper sense, wishes to work for the spread of this threefold impulse must be aware that he has also to take into account spiritual factors like these that are present in human evolution. Indeed the powers on which one must call when one wants to bring something new into the development of humanity are faced not only with the things that any hard-headed philistine notices but also with things that are only laid open to a spiritual knowledge. What use is it when people of today regard this as superstition and do not want to hear that such spiritual beings intrude through human beings? They are nevertheless there, these spiritual beings! And anyone who does not merely want to go through life with a sleeping soul, but with a fully awake soul, can observe the influences of these beings everywhere. If only, from the presence of the effects, people would allow themselves to be convinced a little of the existence of the causes!

This is the characteristic we find when looking towards the West. The West takes on this form because it lives completely in the most fundamental expression of the present epoch – in economic concepts, economic thinking.

The East had once a grand and lofty life of spirit. All spirituality – with the exception of what is striven for in Anthroposophy and is trying to give itself new form – all spirituality of the civilized world is, in actual fact, a legacy of the East. But the real glory of this religious-spiritual life was present in the East only in ancient times. And today the Eastern human being, even in Russia, finds himself in a strange disharmony because on the one hand he still lives in the ancient spiritual element of his heritage and, on the other, there is also working in him that which comes out of the present epoch of human development; namely the training towards becoming an individuality. This brings about a situation such that, in the East, there is a strong decadence in humanity; that, in a sense, the human being cannot become a full human being; that hard on the heels of this Eastern human being, as far west as Russia, is the spiritual heritage of ancient times. And this has the effect that when today the consciousness of this Eastern human being is lowered, when he is in a condition of sleep or dreaming, or in some kind of mediumistic trance state which is so very frequent in the East, he is then, indeed, not entirely impregnated by another being as in the West, but this being works into his soul nature; these beings, as it were, appear to him. Whereas in the West it is premature beings of three kinds that are at work (which I have ennumerated), in the East it is retarded beings, beings that have remained behind from an earlier evolutionary stage of perfection and who now appear to human beings of the East in a mediumistic state, in dreams, or simply during sleep, so that the human being in a waking state then bears within him the inspirations of such beings; is inspired during the day by the after-effects of beings of this kind who come over him during the night.

And here again there are three types of beings working in the East who likewise have a great influence. Whereas in the West one has to draw attention to individual human beings through whom these beings incarnate, in the East one must point to a kind of hierarchy that can appear to the most varied people. Again it is three types of beings; not, however, beings that incarnate through people but beings that appear to people and also inspire them during sleep at night.

The first type of these beings prevents the human being from taking full possession of his physical body, hinders him from finding a connection with the economic element, with the public conditions of the present-day in general. These are the beings who seek in the East to hold back the economic life as it is needed in the threefold social order.

The second type of beings are those that produce over-individualization – a kind of, if I may put it so paradoxically, unegoistic egoism. This is all the more subtle in the way it is so frequently found in people, particularly of the East, who fancifully attribute to themselves all possible selflessness – a selflessness which, however, is in fact a particularly subtle form of self-seeking, a particulary subtle egoism. They want to be absolutely good, they want to be as good as it is ever possible to be. This, too, is an egoistic sentiment. This is something that can be called, paradoxically, an unegoistic egoism, an egoism arising from an imagined selflessness.

The third type of being that appears, in the way described, to human beings of the East are those beings that hold back the spiritual life from the earth; that spread, as it were, a dull mystical atmosphere over human beings, as can be found so frequently today, particularly in the East. And again, these three types of spiritual beings, which work down from the spiritual world and do not incarnate into human beings, are the enemies of the threefold social organism. In this way the threefold impulse is hemmed in from the spiritual side in the East and from the human side, as described, in the West. Thus we see here the spiritual foundations underlying the differentiation.

We still have to add to this what is hostile to the threefolding in the European Centre so that, from a spiritual point of view, we gradually gain an idea of how one must equip oneself in order that the opposing powers – whether from the spiritual world, as in the East, or from human beings, as in the West, or from the Centre of Europe, in a way which I shall relate tomorrow – can be met by the threefold idea with an impulse that is of the greatest conceivable importance for humanity's evolution. And in order to know how one must act with regard to these things one must be equipped with an armour of thoughts.

Dornach, 23 October 1920

Yesterday I drew attention again, but from a different point of view to the one we have taken for some time in the past, to the differentiation that exists among the peoples of the present civilized world. I indicated how the individualization of the human being in the fifth post-Atlantean epoch is guided by spiritual beings: how, on the one side, certain beings interfere through individuals of the West – beings that have progressed in an irregular way, that are more advanced than humanity, but for their own interests incarnate into human beings in order to work against the true impulse of the present, the impulse of the threefolding of the social organism.

I also drew attention to how, in a different way, we find in the East that certain beings, that had their real significance in the far distant past, but wish now to work into and to influence human lives, assert themselves; not, indeed, through human beings themselves, but by appearing to them. We spoke of how these beings influence Eastern human beings, be it more or less consciously, by virtue of the particular soul-configuration of the people living in the Orient; by working as imaginations into the consciousness of certain human beings of the East – perhaps by working during sleep into the human 'I' and astral body – and then asserting themselves, without the people realizing it, in the after-effects during waking. And in this way they bring in everything they wish to pit against the normal progress of humanity in the East. Thus we can say: For a long time in the West a kind of earth-boundness has, in a certain sense, been prepared in such human beings as I described yesterday, who are dispersed there, and who take leading positions, particularly in sects and in secret societies and the like. In the East there are also certain leading personalities who, under the influence of beings from the past who appear to them in imaginations, put into practice in present cultural development what these beings introduce. If one wants to understand how the human beings of the European Centre are wedged in, as it were, between the West and the East one must look more closely into the underlying spiritual conditions and at everything in the physical-sense world that expresses itself out of these spiritual conditions.

I have drawn your attention, from the most varied points of view, to how the life of the ancient Orient was, in the main, a spiritual life; how the human being of the ancient Orient had a highly developed spiritual life that flowed from a direct perception of the spiritual worlds; how this spiritual life then lived on as a heritage; how it existed in Greece, primarily as artistic beauty but also as a certain insight; and how already in Greece there mingled in with it what then became Aristotelianism, what was already intellectual, dialectical thinking. So what came from oriental wisdom penetrated then into Western civilization, and, with the exception of what stems from natural science and what can stem from the modern anthroposophically-oriented spiritual science, everything that exists in Western civilization as spiritual life is basically an inheritance from the ancient Orient. But this spiritual life is, in fact, completely decadent. This spiritual life is of such a nature that it lacks strength, lacks impetus. The human being is, to be sure, guided to the spiritual world through it, but can no longer find a link between what he believes about the spiritual world and what happens here on earth. This shows itself most strongly in Anglo-Saxon Puritanism, in which a faith, completely estranged from the world, has secured itself a place alongside wordly activities. It is directed towards entirely abstract spiritual regions, and basically does not take the trouble to confront and come to terms with the external physical world of the senses.

In the Orient even completely wordly aspirations – aspirations of the social life – take on such a spiritual character that they have the appearance of religious movements. And the momentum of Bolshevism in the East, for example, is to be traced to the fact that it is actually conceived by the people of the East, even by the Russian people, as a religious movement. The impetus of this social movement in the East lies not so much in the abstract concepts of Marxism, but essentially in the fact that its bearers are regarded as new Saviours, as the continuers so to speak, of earlier religious-spiritual striving and life.

From the Roman culture, and even already from the Hellenistic culture there developed, as we know, what took hold of the human beings of the Centre most of all – the dialectical element, the element of political-legal-militaristic thinking. And one can only understand the role played by what then developed out of the Roman culture when one considers at first that all three branches of human experience – the experience of the spiritual, the experience of economics, the experience of the civic-political in which Rome developed to particular splendour and in which the Roman Empire arose – were mixed up and at cross-purposes in much the same way that is the case today over basically the whole civilized world. Rome ended in complete decadence, brought about essentially by the fact that in the Roman Empire the untenable situation arose which always arises when these three human activities – spiritual life, political life and economic life – get mixed up chaotically with one another. It can truly be said that the Roman Empire and particularly the Byzantine Empire were a kind of symbol of the decay of the fourth post-Atlantean epoch, the Graeco-Roman epoch. We need only consider that of 107 Eastern Roman Emperors only 34 died in their beds! The others were either poisoned or maimed and died in prison, or left prison to join monasteries or the like. And out of the decline of the Roman world in Southern Europe developed something which then streamed northwards in three branches (see diagram).

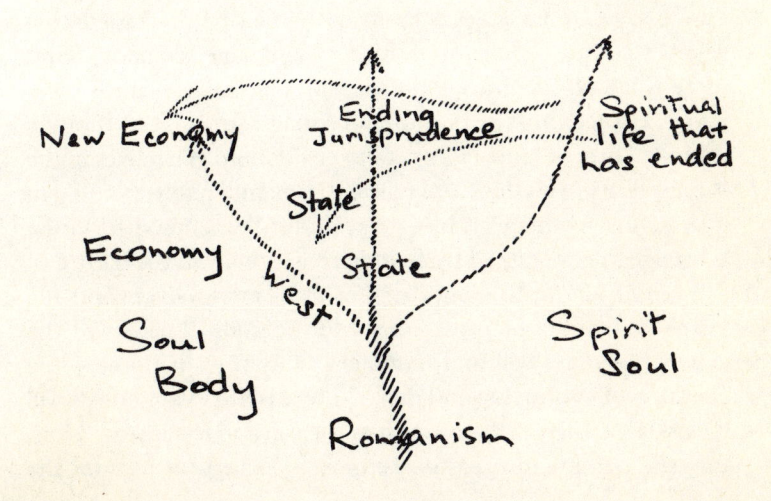

[Diagram: Three branches streaming northwards. Left branch labelled "New Economy" above "Economy / Soul / Body". Middle branch labelled "Ending Jurisprudence / State / State / West" with "Romanism" at the base. Right branch labelled "Spiritual life that has ended / Spirit / Soul".]

Here, to begin with, we have the Western branch. I shall not go today into the historical details of what developed throughout the Middle Ages out of the older development of humanity, but I should like to draw your attention to a few things. The characteristic phenomenon of Western development, of development in the more southerly Western regions to begin with, is that Roman culture spreads as a sum-total of people towards Spain, over present-day France, and also over a part of Britain. These were Roman people who developed in this direction. But all this was interpenetrated by what entered into these Roman peoples through the migrations of Germanic tribes of various kinds.

And here we find a singular phenomenon. We find that Germanic peoples force their way into the Roman element and that something then arises there which can only be characterized by saying: Human beings of Germanic nature penetrated into the Roman element. Rome as such, the Roman human being, went under. But what remained of the Roman culture – what took shape, that is, through the intersection of these two lines (see diagram) and formed the Spanish, the French and also a part of the British population – is essentially Germanic blood overlain by the Roman language-element. It can only really be understood by looking at it in this way. This human being, as regards his soul-configuration, his direction of perceiving, feeling and willing, is descended from what, as the Germanic element, moved in the stream of the migrations from East to West. But it is a peculiarity of this Germanic element that when it comes up against a foreign language element – and there is always a culture embodied in a language – it dissolves into it, assumes it. It grows into this foreign language as though, if I may put it so, into a garment of civilization. What lives in the West of Europe as the Latin race has, fundamentally, nothing in it of Latin blood. But it has grown into what, embodied in the language, has streamed up to it there. For it lay in the nature of the Latin, of the Roman, element to assert itself beyond the purely human in the course of world evolution. This is why the concept of one's will and testament first arose in Rome – the assertion of egoism beyond death. The wish to extend one's will beyond death led to the concept of the will and testament. Thus, too, the continuance of the language worked on beyond the continuance of the human element in the people.

And other things, too, were preserved apart from the language. Thus, in this stream here (see diagram), there was preserved for the West the ancient traditions of the different secret societies, (the significance of which I have frequently referred to in the course of the past years). These are traditions stemming from the fourth post-Atlantean epoch, from the Graeco-Roman times, which, to be sure, are borrowings from the East – from manuscripts – but have passed thoroughly through the Roman, the Latin, culture. Thus, in a certain respect, in so far as Western humanity is submerged in the Roman language-element that has endured beyond the actual Roman people, one finds the human being in the cloak of a foreign civilization. One also has the human being in a foreign cloak in as much as in the ancient Mystery truths – which have become abstract and which, in the ceremonies and ritual of the Western societies, have become more or less empty forms – one has something in which the human element is submerged and which is capable of touching it.

Now, if other conditions are particularly favourable, then this situation [of the human being being penetrated from without by everything that arises from language] provides a foothold for beings of the kind I described yesterday, enabling them to incarnate into the human being. But particularly favourable for this incarnating process is the Anglo-Saxon element. This is because it was a thoroughly Germanic people that moved across to the West and because the Germanic element has been strongly preserved in these human beings who have permeated themselves to a lesser degree with the Roman element than have those whom we call the Latin peoples. Thus there is a far more malleable balance present here in the Anglo-Saxon race, and because of this those beings which incarnate here have far greater freedom of action, far greater room to move in as it were. In the Latin countries proper they would be extremely constricted. Above all, however, one must be clear that what can then manifest in individual personalities depends on configurations of folk psychology such as these. Although Puritanism certainly represented an abstract sphere of belief, this freer Anglo-Saxon element was pre-eminently suited to adopting and developing natural-scientific thinking and to forming a concept of the world and of life based upon it. The whole humanity of the human being, certainly, is not engaged here – only part of man's being is engaged through the incorporation of languages, through the incorporation of other elements of the human being – which makes it possible for such beings as I described yesterday to incarnate in these people.

Let me state expressly that what I am talking about at the moment concerns only certain single individuals who are scattered amongst the mass of other human beings. It does not refer to nations; it does not refer to the vast masses of people but only to single individuals who, however, have an extraordinarily strong position of leadership in those regions I have mentioned. What is primarily taken hold of in the West by these beings, who then secure for the human body in which they incarnate a certain position of leadership, is the body and soul – not the spirit to which less attention is paid.

Where, for example, does the whole magnificent but one-sided elaboration of Charles Darwin's theory of evolution come from?[1] It comes from the fact that, in Charles Darwin, body and soul, and not the spirit, were particularly dominant. He, therefore, also considers the human being only according to body and soul and ignores the spirit and that which lives into the soul from the spirit. Anyone who looks without prejudice at the results of Darwin's research will understand that something was present there which was unwilling to consider the human being from the aspect of his spirit. 'Spirit' was only taken from more recent science – which is international. But what coloured his whole conception of the human being was the emphasis put on body and soul and the disregard for the spirit. In fact, the most faithful pupils of the Ecumenical Council of 869 were the people of the West. Initially they left the spirit out of consideration, taking body and soul in the way they are represented particularly in Darwin's descriptions and simply put an artificial head on top as spirit, in the materialistic way of thinking that arises out of science. And because people were ashamed, as it were, to make a universal religion out of natural science, there remained, as an external appendage, leading an abstract existence of its own, what lived on as Puritanism and the like but which had no connection with the real world culture. We see how here, in a certain sense, body and soul are overwhelmed by an abstract scientific spirit which we can clearly observe even into the present.

But let us suppose that something else happened. Let us suppose that what lives on in language – what lives on in the spiritual world of forms of the fourth post-Atlantean epoch – were to be stronger. What would arise then? There would arise a strong fanatical rejection of the modern spirit; and rather than emphasizing that an 'artificial head' of natural-scientific concepts be superimposed on the bodily-soul element, the old traditions would be superimposed: in fact only the physical and the soul element would really be cultivated. We could then imagine that, in such a crude way, some individual might work on everything that is only body and soul and devise a doctrine that wished only to consider body and soul; which outwardly did not use science for this but rather the external part of a revelation from an earlier time carried over into a later one. And then we have Jesuitism, we have Ignatius of Loyola.[3] We may say that, just as minds like Darwin arose of necessity from Anglo-Saxondom, so from later Romanism there arose Ignatius of Loyola.

The characteristic of the human beings of the West, of whom we have to speak here, is that through them those spiritual beings I described yesterday make themselves felt in the world. In the East this is different. A different stream moves towards the East (see diagram). But we will first look at something that goes out from ancient Rome as a second stream – which does not carry the language but which carries the whole trend of the soul-constitution, the trend of thought. The language goes more to the West and, through this we get all the phenomena of which I have just spoken. The direction of thought, on the other hand, moves more towards the centre of Europe. But it unites there with what lies there with the essential Germanic element; namely, a certain wish to be one with the language. But it is possible to maintain this wish to be one with the language only as long as the people who live in that language remain together. When the Goths, the Vandals and so on moved westwards they were immersed in the Latin element. This 'being one with the language' only remained in the centre of Europe. This means that in Central Europe the language is indeed not bound particularly strongly to human beings but is nevertheless bound more strongly than was the case in the Roman people, who are now lost but who have passed their language on. The Germanic people would not be able to pass on their language. The Germanic people have their language as something living in them and would never be able to leave it behind as a heritage. This language can only continue to live as long as it is bound together with the human being. This is connected with the whole nature of the human constitution of those peoples who have gradually asserted themselves in the centre of Europe. This has the effect that human beings came to the fore in Central Europe who were not suitable for such beings to incarnate into, as was the case in the West. But they could nevertheless be taken hold of. It was quite possible for the beings of the three types I described yesterday to assert themselves in the leaders of the people of Central Europe. But this also makes it possible for those people to be accessible to the phenomena which appear to the people of the Orient as imaginations. But in the people of the Centre these imaginations remain so pale during the day that they appear only as concepts, as ideas. The same applies also to what has its origin in those beings who incarnate in human beings and who play such a great role in individuals of the West. They cannot have the *same* effect here, but nevertheless give the whole human being a certain tendency. It is particularly the case in human beings of the Centre that over the course of centuries it was barely possible for any individual who attained to any sort of significance to save himself from the embodiment of the spirits of the West on the one side, and from the spirits of the East on the other. This always caused a kind of schism in these people.

To describe these human beings [of the Centre] in their true nature we can say: When they were awake there was working in them something of the attacks of the spirits of the West which influenced their desires, their instincts, lived in their will, and crippled it. When these individuals slept, when the astral body and the 'I' were separated, beings asserted themselves in them of the kind that often worked unconsciously on human beings of the Orient, appearing in imaginations. And one only needs to choose a highly characteristic personality from the civilization of the Centre and one will be able to touch – almost, as it were, with one's bare hands – the fact that this is as I have described it.

One only needs to take Goethe. Take everything that lived in Goethe from the attacks of the spirits of the West that asserted themselves in his will, that surged particularly in the young Goethe and which one senses strongly when one reads the scenes, which gushed from Goethe in his youth, of *Faust* or *The Wandering Jew*. And then you see how, on the other hand, Goethe reached calm inner clarity – for the element of the Orient that tends merely to the spirit and soul was mastered in him, was permeated with this will element. You see how in old age he turns, in Part Two of *Faust*, more towards imaginations. But a cleft is nevertheless there. It is difficult to find a bridge between the style of Part One of *Faust* and the style of Part Two.

And look at the living Goethe himself, who grows from the impulses of the West; who, as it were, is tormented by the spirits of the West and who, as a young man, comforts himself with what after all also contains a great deal of the West: the Gothic style. But here there emerges a striving towards the spirits of the past, to those spirits which were at work in Greece – and also, most especially, in the Gothic style – but which nonetheless were basically the successors of those spirits which once inspired the oriental at the time when he came to his great ancient wisdom. And coming to the 1780s we see how he can no longer bear the spirits of the West, how they torment him. And he tries to balance this by moving to the South in order to absorb there what can come from the other side. This is just what gives the leading personalities of the Centre – and the other human beings, of course, follow these leaders – their characteristic stamp. The human beings of the Centre were thereby particularly prepared for the coming to prominence of the one thing that is important for the whole evolution of humanity. One can observe this best in a mind such as Hegel. If you take Hegel's philosophy, you find – I have often mentioned this here – that this philosophy develops in every respect towards the spirit. Yet nowhere in Hegel do you find anything which goes beyond the physical-sense life. Instead of a real teaching on the spirit you find logical dialectics as the first part of his philosophy. His philosophy of nature is merely a sum of abstractions of what lives in the human being himself; and you find what is supposed to be treated by psychology presented in the third part of Hegel's philosophy. But what comes out of it is nothing other than what the human being lives through between birth and death, which is then compressed into history. Nowhere in Hegel is it a matter of the eternal in the human being entering into an existence before birth or after death. Nor can its justification be found anywhere.

This is the one thing that the human beings, the most outstanding human beings, of the Centre give weight to: the fact that the human being, as he lives here between birth and death, consists of body, soul and spirit. For the human beings of the sense-world – for our physical world – soul and spirit should be made manifest by these people of the Centre.

As soon as we move to the East we find that soul and spirit predominate, just as, in the West, it is primarily body and soul. Thus, this rising up to imaginations is natural and, even if they do not come to consciousness, they nevertheless still work into the consciousness. The whole disposition (*Anlage*) of thinking in the human being of the East is such that it tends towards imaginations: even if, at times, these imaginations are taken hold of in abstract concepts, as in Soloviev.[4]

And a third branch extends from Rome towards the North and into the East via Byzantium (see diagram). What was together, though chaotically, in Rome now divides to a certain extent into three separate branches. It diverges and moves to the West where a new element of economics establishes itself as something especially appropriate for the new age, finding close affinity with natural science. It moves also to the East and progresses from the ancient primal wisdom into decadence. There develops that which is the spiritual, in religious form. All this happens, of course, in parallel. And towards the Centre there develops what is political-militaristic, civic-judicial, which also naturally spreads into different areas. But we must keep the characteristic branches in mind.

The further eastward we go, the more do we see how the people of the East are not bound up with their language in the same way that the Germanic peoples are. The Germanic peoples really live in their language as long as they have it. Just study the strange course of the Germanic humanity of Central Europe. Look at the two branches of Germanic population which moved, for example, towards Hungary into the Zipser region; as Swabians down into the Banat; as Siebenbürger

Saxons towards Transylvania. In all these places it is, if I may put it so, rather like a fading away of the actual language element. Everywhere these people allow themselves to be absorbed by the [foreign] language into which they merge. It would be a most interesting ethnological study to see how, in a relatively short time during the last two-thirds of the nineteenth century, the German element in the area around Vienna has withdrawn, has been swamped. This would be tangibly apparent if one looked at this matter with understanding. One saw how the German element evolved into the Magyar in an artificial way and into the Slavonic in a natural way.

In the East the human being is intimately bound up with his language. There the spirit-soul element lives in the language. This is often disregarded. The human being of the West lives in language in a completely different way – in a radically different way – from the human being of the East. The human being of the West lives in his language as though in a garment; the human being of the East lives in his language as though in himself. This is why the human being of the West could adopt the natural-scientific view of life, could pour it into his language, which is only a vessel. The scientific world-view of the West will never find a foothold in the Orient because it simply cannot get into the oriental languages. The languages of the Orient reject it; they do not adopt the world-view of science. You can sense this if you let the – albeit rather coquettish – writings of Rabindranath Tagore[5] work on you. Even though, in Tagore, it is all permeated with coquetry, one nevertheless sees how the whole nature of his existence consists in an experience of the forceful impact of the Western örld-view, and then, through living in the language, an immediate rejection of it.

The human being of the Centre was thrown into all this. He had to take in everything he experienced in the West but did not absorb it as deeply as the Westerner; he suffused it with what also came from the East. Hence the more malleable equilibrium in the Centre; but hence also the inner strife, the duality in the individualization of the souls of human beings of the Centre. The striving to find a harmony, a balancing out of this duality – which is so classicially, so magnificently, portrayed in Schiller's *Letters on Aesthetic Education* in which two driving forces that are to be united – that of Nature and that of Reason

– points clearly to this duality. But one can point to something much deeper. You see, when one looks to the West one finds primarily a certain inclination in the whole people to adopt the natural-scientific way of thinking, which is so exceptionally suited to the economic life. I have shown you how this scientific way of thinking has entered even into psychology. It has been adopted there completely. And it is there that Puritanism lived like an abstract appendage (*Einschlag*), like something that has nothing to do with real outer life – something that one locks away, as it were, in one's soul house – something one does not allow to be touched by outer culture.

The nature of what is developing in the West is such that we can say: There is a tendency here to take into oneself everything that is accessible to human reason in as much as this is bound to body and soul. Everything else – Puritanism – is only the Sunday coat of what is the body, what is accessible to reason. Hence the deism – that squeezed lemon of a religious worldview – in which there is nothing more of God than the fairytale of a generalized, completely abstract, cosmic first cause. Reason, bound to body and soul, is what is asserting itself here.

If you go to the East there is no understanding at all for a rationality of this kind. This already begins in Russia. For, has the Russian any understanding at all for what is called rational in the West? Let us be under no illusion here. The Russian has not the slightest understanding for what, in the West, one calls rationality. The Russian is open to what one could call revelation. Fundamentally, he takes up as the content of his soul everything that comes to him by virtue of a kind of revelation. Reason – even when he says the word, copying it from Western human beings – is something of which he understands nothing; that is, he does not feel in this word what Western people feel. But what can be felt when one speaks of revelations, of the descent of truths from the supersensible worlds into human beings – this he understands well. Through the nature of what is spoken of in the West – and Puritanism is indeed good proof of this – one sees that there is by nature not the slightest understanding for what one must refer to as the relation of the Russian – and even more so of the oriental, of the Asiatic human being – of the relation in general of the human being to the spiritual world. In the West there is not the slightest understanding for this. For this is something quite different from what is given through reason. It is something which, going out from the spirit, takes hold of the human being and permeates him in a living way.

And in the human being of Central Europe the situation is this: as the fifth post-Atlantean epoch was approaching — around the tenth, eleventh and twelfth centuries (it came then in the fifteenth century) — the outstanding spirits of Central Europe were faced with an immense question, a question that was set them as human beings placed between West and East — a West that pulled them towards reason and an East that pulled them towards revelation. Just study later Scholasticism, the brilliant age of medieval spiritual development, from this point of view. Just study, from this standpoint, such spirits as Albertus Magnus,[6] Thomas Aquinas,[7] Duns Scotus[8] and so on. Compare them with such spirits as Roger Bacon[9] — I mean the elder, who was more orientated towards the West — and you will see that a great question arose for the spirits of later Central-European Scholasticism, from the working together of what pressed in from the West as reason and what pressed in from the East as revelation. This pressure came, on the one hand, from those spirits who wished to take hold of the human body and soul through the will and from those spirits, on the other hand, who, in the East, wished to take hold of spirit and soul through imaginations. It is from this that the tenet of Scholastic teaching arose that both were valid: reason on the one side and revelation on the other. Reason for everything on the earth which can be acquired through the senses and revelation for the supersensible truths which can be drawn only from the Bible and from the traditions of Christianity. One comprehends the Christian Scholasticism of the Middle Ages when one perceives its most outstanding spirits as being those in whom reason from the West and revelation from the East came together. Both influences were working in the human being and in the Middle Ages people could only bring them together by feeling the split, the duality in themselves.

In that place high up in the small cupola,[10] where the Germanic element is meant to be shown with its dualism, you see the elements of this duality clashing against one another in the red-yellow and the black-brown — the red-yellow of revelation and the black-brown of reason. You see there, felt in colour, revealed through colour, what has inspired and worked through different human cultures and has thus come to the human being.

Thus we could say that what we have now, spread over the civilized world, is taken hold of in the West by economic life – the element that has actually arisen only in modern times. For economic life was never such a topical question in earlier epochs as it is today. It is actually appropriate to our times. In contrast, matters of state and politics are already fading. And what was founded in the last third of the nineteenth century as the German Empire took into itself just this fading element of ancient Rome and fell to pieces because of it. This was already so at the beginning in the way it was structured but even more so in the way it then developed. Fundamentally, this German Empire was nothing but a continuation of the civic-judicial, the political element, which excelled in organizing everything – indeed, had great geniuses of organization. But it wanted to also take over the economic life without having economic thinking. For everything that the economy did in this Empire wanted more and more to creep under the umbrella of the State. Militarism, for example, which basically orginated in France and also in Switzerland but which had quite different forms, was 'politicized' (*verstaatlicht*), as it were, in Central Europe. Central Europe could therefore take up neither an economic life nor a spiritual life truly alive in itself and arising out of its own roots. The anti-spirituality that has been organized in Central Europe in recent times is of the most terrible kind! We see everything pertaining to the spiritual life becoming more and more part of a political State. And so it came about that in Central Europe in the second decade of the twentieth century there was not a single individual left who wrote about history or similar things except as a 'party-political man'. Everything which came out of the universities was not objective history but party-wisdom, distinctly politically coloured. And even more decadent is the spiritual life which originates in very ancient times in the Orient. It mingled with the deluge from the West, from the Centre, in the measures of Peter the Great with the native spirituality that was already in a state of decadence, expressing itself in Pan-Slavism, in Slavophilism. And it led finally to the creation of the present conditions from which a new spirit wishes to arise, for the old is completely decadent.

Thus we see, spread out over the world, a new economy, jurisprudence and political life coming to an and, and a spiritual life which has come to an end.

In the West we see how the political element has been completely absorbed by the economy and that the spiritual element, if one disregards the unreality of Puritanism, exists only in the form of natural science. In the Centre we have had an already ageing State which tried to absorb both economy and spiritual life and was therefore unable to survive. And in the East we have nothing but the dying spirit of ancient times which the West tries to galvanize through all manner of measures. No matter whether tried by Peter the Great or by Lenin, what wishes to come from the West galvanizes the corpse of the Eastern spirit. Salvation lies in clearly seeing that a *new* spirit must permeate humanity.

This new spirit, which cannot be found in the Orient but only in the Occident, must put economic life, political life and spiritual life side by side, quite distinct from one another. Then the economic life of the West, for which the West is particularly organized through its natural qualities, can be complemented by the political and the spiritual life. Then the Centre can take up beside its political life – which will be improved through quite different principles than were there in the past if it is anthroposophically-oriented – an economic and spiritual life. And then the Orient can be re-fructified. The Orient will understand the spiritual life that blossoms in the Occident only if one introduces it in the right way. As soon as artificial barriers are no longer created, which do not allow the movement of the truly anthroposophically-oriented spiritual life of the Occident; as soon as this is allowed to cross into the Orient, it will be understood there, even if it enters at first through such coquettish spirits as Rabindranath Tagore or others. The point is that natural science as such is rejected by the Orient. But that science which is illumined by true spirituality, which we have wanted to present here in our courses of the Free School of Spiritual Science, will also be taken up in the Orient with great eagerness. The Orient will then have a great deal of understanding for an independent spiritual life. And it will also take up an independent civic-political life and an independent economic life which it will be able to run in independence. Thus, in this threefold form of the social organism, there is a fulfillment of that which, from a rational but at the same time also spiritual view, represents the development of the European and Asiatic world since the decline of Rome.

Dornach, 24 October 1920

As early as 1891 I drew attention[1] to the relation between Schiller's *Aesthetic Letters*[2] and Goethe's *Fairy-tale of the Green Snake and the Beautiful Lily*.[3] I would like today to point to a certain connection between what I gave yesterday as the characteristic of the civilization of the Central-European countries in contrast to the Western and Eastern ones and what arises in quite a unique way in Goethe and Schiller. I characterized, on the one hand, the seizure of the human corporality by the spirits of the West and, on the other hand, the feeling of those spiritual beings who, as imaginations, as spirits of the East, work inspiringly into Eastern civilization. And one can notice both these aspects in the leading personalities of Goethe and Schiller. I will only point out in addition how in Schiller's *Aesthetic Letters* he seeks to characterize a human soul-constitution which shows a certain middle mood between one possibility in the human being – his being completely given over to instincts, to the sensible-physical – and the other possibility – that of being given over to the logical world of reason. Schiller holds that, in both cases, the human being cannot come to freedom. For if he has completely surrendered himself to the world of the senses, to the world of instincts, of desires, he is given over to his bodily-physical nature and is unfree. But he is also unfree when he surrenders himself completely to the necessity of reason, to logical necessity; for then he is coerced under the tyranny of the laws of logic. But Schiller wants to point to a middle state in which the human being has spiritualized his instincts to such a degree that he can give himself up to them without their dragging him down, without their enslaving him, and in which, on the other hand, logical necessity is taken up into sense perception (*sinnliche Anschauen*), taken up into personal desires (*Triebe*), so that these logical necessities do not also enslave the human being.

Schiller finds this middle state in the condition of aesthetic enjoyment and aesthetic creation, in which the human being can come to true freedom.

It is an extremely important fact that Schiller's whole treatise arose out of the same European mood as did the French Revolution. The same thing which, in the West, expressed itself tumultuously as a large political movement orientated towards external upheaval and change also moved Schiller – but moved him in such a way that he sought to answer the question: What must the human being do in himself in order to become a truly free being? In the West they asked: How must the external social conditions be changed so that the human being can become free? Schiller asked: What must the human being become in himself so that, in his constitution of soul, he can live in (*darleben*) freedom? And he sees that if human beings are educated to this middle mood they will also represent a social community governed by freedom. Schiller thus wishes to realize a social community in such a way that free conditions are created through [the inner nature of] human beings and not through outer measures.

Schiller came to this composition of his *Aesthetic Letters* through his schooling in Kantian philosophy. His was indeed a highly artistic nature, but in the 1780s and the beginning of the 1790s he was strongly influenced by Kant and tried to answer such questions for himself in a Kantian way (*im Kantischen Sinne*). Now the *Aesthetic Letters* were written just at the time when Goethe and Schiller were founding the magazine *Die Horen (The Hours)* and Schiller lays the *Aesthetic Letters* before Goethe.

Now we know that Goethe's soul-configuration was quite different from Schiller's. It was precisely because of the difference of their soul-constitutions that these two became so close. Each could give to the other just that which the other lacked. Goethe now received Schiller's *Aesthetic Letters* in which Schiller wished to answer the question: How can the human being come inwardly to a free inner constitution of soul and outwardly to free social conditions? Goethe could not make much of Schiller's philosophical treatise. This way of presenting concepts, of developing ideas, was not unfamiliar to him. Anyone who, like myself, has seen how Goethe's own copy of Kant's *Critique of Pure Reason* is filled with underlinings and marginal comments knows how Goethe had really studied this work of Kant's which was abstract, but in a completely different sense. And just as he seems to have been able to take works such as these purely as study material, so, of course, he could also have taken Schiller's *Aesthetic Letters*. But this was not the point. For Goethe this whole construction of the human being – on the one hand logical necessity and on the other the senses with their sensual needs, as Schiller said, and the third, the middle condition – for Goethe this was all far too cut and dried, far too simplistic. He felt that one could not picture the human being so simply, or present human development so simply, and thus he wrote to Schiller that he did not want to treat the problem, this whole riddle, in such a philosophical, intellectual form, but more pictorially. Goethe then treated this same problem in picture form – as reply, as it were, to Schiller's *Aesthetic Letters* – in his *Fairy-tale of the Green Snake and the Beautiful Lily* by presenting the two realms on this and on the far side of the river, in a pictorial, rich and concrete way; the same thing that Schiller presents as sense-life and the life of reason. And what Schiller characterizes abstractly as the middle condition, Goethe portrays in the building of the temple in which rule the King of Wisdom (the Golden King), the King of Semblance (the Silver King), the King of Power (the Copper King) and in which the Mixed King falls to pieces. Goethe wanted to deal with this in a pictorial way. And we have, in a certain sense, an indication – but in the Goethean way – of the fact that the outer structure of human society must not be monolithic but must be a threefoldness if the human being is to thrive in it. What in a later epoch had to emerge as the threefold social order is given here by Goethe still in the form of an image. Of course, the threefold social order does not yet exist but Goethe gives the form he would like to ascribe to it in these three kings; in the Golden, the Silver, and the Copper King. And what cannot hold together he gives in the Mixed King.

But it is no longer possible to give things in this way. I have shown this in my first Mystery Drama[4] which, in essence, deals with the same theme but in the way required by the beginning of the twentieth century, whereas Goethe wrote his *Fairy-tale* at the end of the eighteenth century.

Now, however, it is already possible to indicate in a certain way – even though Goethe had not himself yet done so – how the Golden King would correspond to that aspect of the social organism which we call the spiritual aspect: how the King of Semblance, the Silver King, would correspond to the political State: how the King of Power, the Copper King, would correspond to the economic aspect, and how the Mixed King, who disintegrates, represents the 'Uniform State' which can have no permanence in itself.

This was how, in images, Goethe pointed to what would have to arise as the threefold social order. Goethe thus said, as it were, when he received Schiller's *Aesthetic Letters*: One cannot do it like this. You, dear friend, picture the human being far too simplistically. You picture three forces. This is not how it is with the human being. If one wishes to look at the richly differentiated inner nature of the human being, one finds about twenty forces – which Goethe then presents in his twenty archetypal fairy-tale figures – and one must then portray the interplay and interaction of these twenty forces in a much less abstract way.

Thus at the end of the eighteenth century we have two presentations of the same thing. One by Schiller, from the intellect as it were, though not in the usual way that people do things from the intellect, but such that the intellect is permeated here with feeling and soul, is permeated by the whole human being. Now there is a difference between some dry, average, professional philistine presenting something on the human being in psychological terms, where only the head thinks about the matter, and Schiller, out of an experience of the whole human being, forming for himself the ideal of a human constitution of soul and thereby only transforming into intellectual concepts what he actually feels.

It would be impossible to go further on the path taken by Schiller using logic or intellectual analysis without becoming philistine and abstract. In every line of these *Aesthetic Letters* there is still the full feeling and sensibility of Schiller. It is not the stiff Königsberg approach of Immanuel Kant with dry concepts; it is profundity in intellectual form transformed into ideas. But should one take it just one step further one would come into the intellectual mechanism that is realized in the usual science of today in which, basically, behind what is structured and developed intellectually, the human being has no more significance. It thus becomes a matter of no importance whether Professor A or D or X deals with the subject because what is presented does not arise from the whole human being. In Schiller everything still has a totally personal (*urpersönlich*) nature, even into the intellect. Schiller lives there in a phase – indeed, in an evolutionary point of the modern development of humanity which is of essential importance – because Schiller stops just short of something into which humanity later fell completely.

Let us show diagramatically what might be meant here. One could say: This is the general tendency of human evolution (arrow pointing upwards). Yet it cannot go [straight] like this – portrayed only schematically – but loops round into a lemniscate (blue). But it cannot go on like that – there must, if evolution takes this course, be continually new impulses (*Antriebe*) which move the lemniscates up along the line.

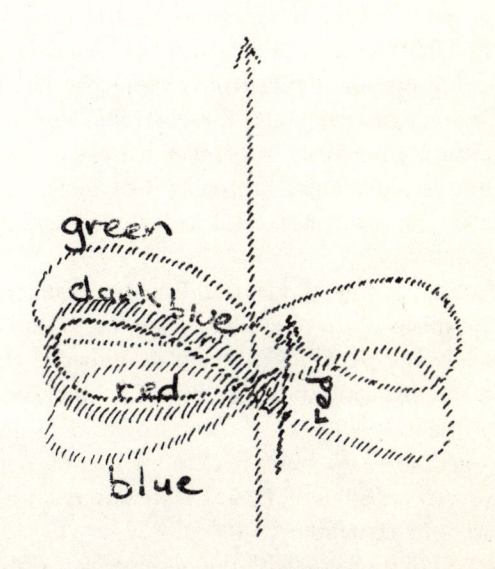

Schiller, having arrived at this point here (see diagram), would have gone into a dark blue, as it were, of mere abstraction, of intellectuality, had he proceeded further in objectifying what he felt inwardly. But he drew a halt and paused with his forms of reasoning just at that point at which the personality is not lost. Thus, this did not become blue but, on a higher level of the personality – which I will colour with red (see diagram) – was

61

turned into green.

Thus one can say: Schiller held back with his intellectuality just before that point at which intellectuality tries to emerge in its purity. Otherwise he would have fallen into the usual intellect of the nineteenth century. Goethe expressed the same thing in images, in wonderful images, in his *Fairy-tale of the Green Snake and the Beautiful Lily*. But he, too, stopped at the images. He could not bear these pictures to be in any way criticized because, for him, what he perceived and felt about the individual human element and the social life, did simply present itself in such pictures. But he was allowed to go no further than these images. For had he, from his standpoint, tried to go further he would have come into wild, fantastic daydreams. The subject would no longer have had definite contours; it would no longer have been applicable to real life but would have risen above and beyond it. It would have become rapturous fantasy. One could say that Goethe had to avoid the other chasm, in which he would have come completely into a fantastic red. Thus he adds that element which is non-personal – that which keeps the pictures in the realm of the imaginative – and thereby came also to the green.

Expressing it schematically, Schiller had, as it were, avoided the blue, the Ahrimanic-intellectuality; Goethe had avoided the red, excessive rapturousness, and kept to concrete imaginative pictures.

As a human being of Central Europe, Schiller had confronted the spirits of the West. They wanted to lead him astray into the solely intellectual. Kant had succumbed to this. I spoke about this recently[5] and indicated how Kant had succumbed to the intellectuality of the West through David Hume. Schiller had managed to work himself clear of this even though he allowed himself to be taught by Kant. He stayed at the point that is not mere intellectuality.

Goethe had to do battle with the other spirits, with the spirits of the East, who pulled him towards imaginations. Because at that time spiritual science was not yet present on the earth he could not go further than to the web of imaginations in the *Fairy-tale of the Green Snake and the Beautiful Lily*. But even here he managed to remain within firm contours. He did not go off into wild fantasy or ecstasies. He gave himself a new and fruitful stimulus through his journey to the South where much of the legacy from the Orient was still preserved. He learnt how the spirits of the East still worked here as a late blossoming of oriental culture; in Greek art as he construed this for himself from Italian works of art. It can therefore be said that there was something quite unique in this bond of friendship between Schiller and Goethe. Schiller had to battle with the spirits of the West; he did not yield to them but held back and did not fall into mere intellectuality. Goethe had to battle with the spirits of the East; they tried to pull him into ecstatic reveries (*zum Schwärmerischen*). He, too, held back; he kept to the images which he gives in his *Fairy-tale of the Green Snake and the Beautiful Lily*. Goethe would have had either to succumb to rapturous daydreams (*Schwärmerei*) or to take up oriental revelation. Schiller would have had either to become completely intellectual or would have had to take seriously what he became – it is well known that he was made a 'French citizen' by the revolutionary government but that he did not take the matter very seriously.

We see here how, at an important point of European development, these two soul-constitutions, which I have characterized for you, stand side by side. They live anyway, so to speak, in every significant Central-European individuality but in Schiller and Goethe they stand in a certain way simultaneously side by side. Schiller and Goethe remained, as it were, at this point, for it just required the intercession of spiritual science to raise the curve of the lemniscate (see diagram) to a higher level.

And thus, in a strange way, in Schiller's three conditions – the condition of the necessity of reason, the condition of the necessity of instincts and that of the free aesthetic mood – and in Goethe's three kings – the Golden King, the Silver King, and the Copper King – we see a prefiguration of everything that we must find through spiritual science concerning the threefold nature of the human being as well as the threefold differentiation of the social community representing, as these do, the most immediate and essential aims and problems of the individual human being and of the way human beings live together.

These things direct us indeed to the fact that this threefolding of the social organism is not brought to the surface arbitrarily but that even the finest spirits of modern human evolution have already moved in this direction. But if there were only the ideas about the social questions such as those in Goethe's *Fairy-tale* and nothing more one would never come to an impetus for actual outer action. Goethe was at the point of overcoming mere revelations. In Rome he did not become a Catholic but raised himself up to his imaginations. But he stopped there, with just pictures. And Schiller did not become a revolutionary but a teacher of the inner human being. He stopped at the point where intellect is still suffused with the personality.

Thus, in a later phase of European culture, there was still something at work which can be perceived also in ancient times and most clearly, for modern people, in the culture of ancient Greece. Goethe also strove towards this Greek element. In Greece one can see how the social element is presented in myth – that is, also in picture form. But the Greek myth, basically, is image in the same way that Goethe's *Fairy-tale* is image. It is not possible with these images to work into the social organism in a reforming way. One can only describe as an idealist, as it were, what ought to take shape. But the images are too frail a structure to enable one to act strongly and effectively in the shaping of the social organism. For this very reason the Greeks did not believe that their social questions were met by remaining in the images of the myths. And it is here, when one follows this line of investigation, that one comes to an important point in Greek development.

One could put it like this: for everyday life, where things go on in the usual way, the Greeks considered themselves dependant on their gods, on the spirits of their myths. When, however, it was a matter of deciding something of great importance, then the Greeks said: Here it is not those gods who work into imaginations and are the gods of the myths that can determine the matter; here something real must come to light. And so the Oracle arose. The gods were not pictured here merely imaginatively but were called upon (*veranlasst*) really to inspire people. And it was with the sayings of the Oracle that the Greeks concerned themselves when they wanted to receive social impulses. Here they ascended from imagination to inspiration, but an inspiration which they attained by means of outer nature. We modern human beings must certainly also endeavour to lift ourselves up to inspiration; an inspiration, however, that does not call upon outer nature in oracles but which rises to the spirit in order to be inspired in the sphere of the spirit. But just as the Greeks turned to reality in matters of the social sphere – just as they did not stop at imaginations but ascended to inspirations – so we, too, cannot stop at imaginations but must rise up to inspirations if we are to find anything for the well-being of human society in the modern age.

And we come here to another point which is important to look at. Why did Schiller and Goethe both stop at a certain point – the one on the path towards the intellectual (*Verständiges*) and the other on the path to the imaginative? Neither of them had spiritual science; otherwise Schiller would have been able to advance to the point of permeating his concepts in a spiritual-scientific way and he would then have found something much more real in his three soul-conditions than the three abstractions in his *Aesthetic Letters*. Goethe would have filled imagination with what speaks out in all reality from the spiritual world and would have been able to penetrate to the forms of the social life which wish to be put into effect from the spiritual world – to the spiritual element in the social organism, the Golden King; to the political element in the social organism, the Silver King; and to the economic element, the Bronze, the Copper, King.

The age in which Goethe and Schiller pressed forward to these insights – the one in the *Aesthetic Letters* and the other in the *Fairy-tale* – was not yet able to go any further. For, in order to penetrate further, there is something quite definite that must first be realized. People have to see what becomes of the world if one continues along Schiller's path up to the full elaboration (*Ausgestaltung*) of the impersonally intellectual. The nineteenth century developed it to being with in natural science and the second half of the nineteenth century already began to try to realize it in outer public affairs. There is a significant secret here. In the human organism what is ingested is also finally destroyed. We cannot simply go on eating but must also excrete; the substance we take in has to meet with destruction, has to be destroyed, and has then to leave the organism. And the intellectual is that which – and here comes a complication – as soon as it gets hold of the economic life in the uniform State, in the Mixed King, destroys that economic life.

But we are now living in the time in which the intellect must evolve. We could not come to the development of the consciousness-soul in the fifth post-Atlantean epoch without developing the intellect. And it is the Western peoples that have just this task of bringing the intellect into the economic life. What does this mean? We cannot order modern economic life imaginatively, in the way that Goethe did in his *Fairy-tale*, because we have to shape it through the intellect (*verständig*). Because in economics we cannot but help to go further along the path which Schiller took, though in his case he went only as far as the still-personal outbreathing of the intellect. We have to establish an economic life which, because it has to come from the intellect, of necessity works destructively in the fifth post-Atlantean epoch. In the present age there is no economic life that could be run imaginatively like that of the Orient or the economy of medieval Europe. Since the middle of the fifteenth century we have only had the possibility of an economic life which, whether existing alone or mixed with the other limbs of the social organism, works destructively. There is no other way. Let us therefore look on this economic life as the side of the scales that would sink far down and therefore has to work destructively. But there also has to be a balance. For this reason we must have an economic life that is one part of the social organism, and a spiritual life which holds the balance, which builds up again. If one clings today to the uniform State, the economic life will absorb this uniform State together with the spiritual life, and uniform States like these must of necessity lead to destruction. And when, like Lenin and Trotsky, one founds a State purely out of the intellect it must lead to destruction because the intellect is directly solely to the economic life.

This was felt by Schiller as he thought out his social conditions. Schiller felt: If I go further in the power of the intellect (*verständesmässiges Können*) I will come into the economic life and will have to apply the intellect to it. I will not then be portraying what grows and thrives but what lives in destruction. Schiller shrank back before the destruction. He stopped just at the point where destruction would break in. People of today invent all sorts of social economic systems but are not aware, because they lack the sensitivity of feeling for it, that every economic system like this that they think up leads to destruction; leads definitely to destruction if it is not constantly renewed by an independent, developing spiritual life which ever and ever again works as a constructive element in relation to the destruction, the excretion, of the economic life. The working together of the spiritual limb of the social organism with the economic element is described in this sense in my *Towards Social Renewal* (*Kernpunkte der Sozialen Frage*).[6]

If, with the modern intellectuality of the fifth post-Atlantean epoch, people were to hold on to capital even when they themselves could no longer manage it, the economic life itself would cause it to circulate. Destruction would inevitably have to come. This is where the spiritual life has to intervene; capital must be transferred via the spiritual life to those who are engaged in its administration. This is the inner meaning of the threefolding of the social organism; namely that, in a properly thought out threefold social organism, one should be under no illusion that the economic thinking of the present is a destructive element which must, therefore, be continually counterbalanced by the *constructive* element of the spiritual limb of the social organism.

In every generation, in the children whom we teach at school, something is given to us; something is sent down from the spiritual world. We take hold of this in education – this is something spiritual – and incorporate it into the economic life and thereby ward off its destruction. For the economic life, if it runs its own course, destroys itself. This is how we must look at things. Thus we must see how at the end of the eighteenth century there stood Goethe and Schiller. Schiller said to himself: I must pull back, I must not describe a social system which calls merely on the personal intellect. I must keep the intellect within the personality, otherwise I would describe economic destruction. And Goethe: I want sharply contoured images, not excessive vague ones. For if I were to go any further along that path I would come into a condition that is not on the earth, that does not take hold with any effect on life itself. I would leave the economic life below me like something lifeless and would found a spiritual life that is incapable of reaching into the immediate circumstances of life.

Thus we are living in true Goetheanism when we do not stop at Goethe but also share the development in which Goethe himself took part since 1832. I have indicated this fact – that the economic life today continually works towards its own destruction and that this destruction must be continually counterbalanced. I have indicated this in a particular place in my *Towards Social Renewal*. But people do not read things properly. They think that this book is written in the same way most books are written today – that one can just read it through. Every sentence in a book such as this, written out of practical insight, requires to be thoroughly thought through!

But if one takes these two things [Goethe's *Fairy-tale* and Schiller's *Aesthetic Letters*], Schiller's *Aesthetic Letters* were little understood in the time that followed them. I have often spoken about this. People gave them little attention. Otherwise the study of Schiller's *Aesthetic Letters* would have been a good way of coming into what you find in my *Knowledge of the Higher Worlds – How is it Achieved?* Schiller's *Aesthetic Letters* would be a good preparation for this. And likewise, Goethe's *Fairy-tale* could also be the preparation for acquiring that configuration of thinking (*Geisteskonfiguration*) which can arise not merely from the intellect but from still deeper forces, and which would be really able to understand something like *Towards Social Renewal*. For both Schiller and Goethe sensed something of the tragedy of Central European civilization – certainly not consciously, but they sensed it nevertheless. Both felt – and one can read this everywhere in Goethe's conversations with Eckermann, with Chancellor von Müller, and in numerous other comments by Goethe – that if something like a new impulse from the spirit did not arise, like a new comprehension of Christianity, then everything must go into decline. A great deal of the resignation which Goethe felt in his later years is based, without doubt, on this mood.

And those who, without spiritual science, have become Goetheanists feel how, in the very nature of German Central Europe, this singular working side by side of the spirits of the West and the spirits of the East is particularly evident. I said yesterday that in Central European civilization the balance sought by later Scholasticism between rational knowledge and revelation is attributable to the working of the spirits of the West and the spirits of the East. We have seen today how this shows itself in Goethe and Schiller. But, fundamentally, the whole of Central European civilization wavers in the whirlpool in which

East and West swirl and interpenetrate one another. From the East the sphere of the Golden King; from the West the sphere of the Copper King. From the East, Wisdom; from the West, Power. And in the middle is what Goethe represented in the Silver King, in Semblance; that which imbues itself with reality only with great difficulty. It was this semblance-nature of Central European civilization which lay as the tragic mood at the bottom of Goethe's soul. And Herman Grimm, who also did not know spiritual science, gave in a beautiful way, out of his sensitive feeling for Goethe whom he studied, a fine characterization of Central-European civilization. He saw how it had the peculiarity of being drawn into the whirlpool of the spirits of the East and the spirits of the West. This has the effect of preventing the will from coming into its own and leads to the constantly vacillating mood of German history. Herman Grimm[8] puts it beautifully when he says: 'To Treitschke German history is the incessant striving towards spiritual and political unity and, on the path towards this, the incessant interference by our own deepest inherent peculiarities.' This is what Herman Grimm says, experiencing himself as a German. And he describes this further as 'Always the same way in our nature to oppose where we should give way and to give way where resistance is called for. The remarkable forgetting of what has just past. Suddenly no longer wanting what, a moment ago, was vigorously striven for. A disdain for the present, but strong, indefinite hope. Added to this the tendency to give ourselves over to the foreigner and, no sonner having done so, then exercising an unconscious, determining (*massgebende*) influence on the foreigners to whom we had subjected ourselves.'

When, today, one has to do with Central European civilization and would like to arrive at something through it, one is everywhere met by the breath of this tragic element which is betrayed by the whole history of the German, the Central European element, between East and West. It is everywhere still so today that, with Herman Grimm, one can say: There is the urge to resist where one should give way and to give way where resistance is needed.

This is what arises from the vacillating human beings of the Centre; from what, between economics and the reconstructing spirit-life, stands in the middle as the rhythmical oscillating to and fro of the political. Because the civic-political element has celebrated its triumph in these central countries, it is here that a semblance lives which can easily become illusion. Schiller, in writing his *Aesthetic Letters*, did not want to abandon semblance. He knew that where one deals purely with the intellect, one comes into the destruction of the economic life. In the eighteenth century that part was destroyed which could be destroyed by the French Revolution; in the nineteenth century it would be much worse. Goethe knew that he must not go into wild fantasies but keep to true imagination. But in the vacillation between the two sides of this duality, which arises in the swirling, to and fro movement of the spirits of the West and of the East, there is easily generated an atmosphere of illusion. It does not matter whether this illusionary atmosphere emerges in religion, in politics or in militarism; in the end it is all the same whether the ecstatic enthusiast produces some sort of mysticism or enthuses in the way Ludendorff[9] did without standing on the ground of reality. And, finally, one can also meet it in a pleasing way. For the same place in Herman Grimm which I just read out continues as follows: 'You can see it today: no one seemed to be so completely severed from their homeland as the Germans who became Americans, and yet American life, into which our emigrants dissolved, stands today under the influence of the German spirit.'

Thus writes the brilliant Herman Grimm in 1895 when it was only out of the worst illusion that one could believe that the Germans who went to America would give American life a German colouring. For already, long before this, there had been prepared what then emerged in the second decade of the twentieth century: that the American element completely submerged what little the Germans had been able to bring in.

And the illusionary nature of this remark by Herman Grimm becomes all the greater when one finally bears in mind the following. Herman Grimm makes this comment from a Goethean way of thinking (*Gesinnung*), for he had modelled himself fully on Goethe. But he had a certain other quality. Anyone who knows Herman Grimm more closely knows that in his style, in his whole way of expressing himself, in his way of thinking, he had absorbed a great deal of Goethe, but not

Goethe's real and penetrating quality – for Grimm's descriptions are such that what he actually portrays are shadow pictures, not real human beings. But he has something else in him, not just Goethe. And what is it that Herman Grimm has in himself? Americanism! For what he had in his style, in his thought-forms, apart from Goethe he has from early readings of Emerson. Even his sentence structure, his train of thought, is copied from the American, Emerson.[10]

Thus, Herman Grimm is under this double illusion, in the realm of the Silver King of Semblance. At a time when all German influence has been expunged from America he fondly believes that America has been Germanized, when in fact he himself has quite a strong vein of Americanism in him.

Thus there is often expressed in a smaller, more intimate context what exists in a less refined form in external culture at large. A crude Darwinism, a crude economic thinking, has spread out there and would in the end, if the threefolding of the social organism fails to come, lead to ruin – for an economic life constructed purely intellectually must of necessity lead to ruin. And anyone who, like Oswald Spengler,[11] thinks in the terms of this economic life can prove scientifically that at the beginning of the third millenium the modern civilized world – which today is actually no longer so very civilized – will have had to sink into the most desolate barbarity. For Spengler knows nothing of what the world must receive as an impulse, as a spiritual impulse.

But the spiritual science and the spiritual-scientific culture which not only wishes to enter, but *must* enter, the world today still has an extremely difficult task getting through. And everywhere those who wish to prevent this spiritual science from arising assert themselves. And, basically, there are only a few energetic workers in the field of spiritual science whereas the others, who lead into the works of destruction, are full of energy.

One only has to see how people of today are actually completely at a loss in the face of what comes up in the life of present civilization. It is characteristic, for instance, how a newspaper of Eastern Switzerland carried articles on my lectures on *The Boundaries of Natural Science* during the course at the School of Spiritual Science. And now, in the town where the newspaper is published, Arthur Drews[12], the copy-cat of Eduard von Hartmann, holds lectures in which he has never done anything more than rehash Eduard von Hartmann, the philosopher of the unconscious.[13] In the case of Hartmann it is interesting. In the case of the rehasher it is, of course, highly superfluous. And this philosophical hollow-headedness working at Karlsruhe University is now busying itself with anthroposophically-orientated spiritual science.

And how does the modern human being — I would particularly like to emphasize this — confront these things? Well, we have listened to one person, we now go and listen to someone else. This means that, for the modern human being, it is all a matter of indifference, and this is a terrible thing. Whether the rehasher of Eduard von Hartmann, Arthur Drews, has something against Anthroposophy or not is not the important point — for what the man can have against Anthroposophy can be fully construed beforehand from his books, not a single sentence need be left out. The significant thing is that people's standpoint is that one hears something, makes a note of it, and then it is over and done with, finished! All that is needed to come to the right path is that people really go into the matter. But people today do not want to be taken up with having to go into something properly. This is the really terrible and awful thing; this is what has already pushed people so far that they are no longer able to distinguish between what is speaking of realities and what writes whole books, like those of Count Hermann Von Keyserling,[14] in which there is not one single thought, just jumbled-together words. And when one longs for something to be taken up enthusiastically — which would, of itself, lead to this hollow word-skirmishing being distinguished from what is based on genuine spiritual research — one finds no one who rouses himself, makes a stout effort and is able to be taken hold of by that which has substance. This is what people have forgotten — and forgotten thoroughly — in this age in which truth is not decided according to truth itself, but in which the great lie walks among men so that in recent years individual nations have only found to be true what comes from them and have found what comes from other nations to be false. The disgusting way that people lie to each other has fundamentally become the stamp of the public spirit. Whenever something came from another nation it was deemed untrue. If it came from one's own nation it was true. This still echoes on today; it has already become a habit of thought. In contrast, a genuine, unprejudiced devotion to truth leads to spiritualization. But this is basically still a matter of indifference for modern human beings.

Until a sufficiently large number of people are willing to engage themselves absolutely whole-heartedly for spiritual science, nothing beneficial will come from the present chaos. People should not believe that one can somehow progress by galvanizing the old. This 'old' founds 'Schools of Wisdom' on purely hollow words. It has furnished university philosophy with the Arthur Drews's who, however, are actually represented everywhere, and yet humanity will not take a stand. Until it takes a stand in all three spheres of life – in the spiritual, the political and the economic spheres – no cure can come out of the present-day chaos. It must sink ever deeper!

Dornach, 29 October 1920

The subject about which I shall have to speak today, tomorrow and the day after tomorrow, and which was already referred to some time ago,[1] is the special way in which, in the first half of the twentieth century, a kind of renewed manifestation of the Christ-Event is to take place. This will need a certain amount of preparation, and today, to begin with, I shall try to characterize again from a certain point of view the spiritual complexion of the civilized world and, from this point of view, draw attention to the challenges that are placed before us with regard to the evolution of humanity – the education of humanity as a whole in the near future – by the facts of this human evolution itself.

We know that a new age in the development of civilized humanity began around the beginning of the fifteenth century. People today no longer form an exact idea of what the constitution of soul was like in the people who lived before this great turning-point of modern history. People do not consider this. But one could easily imagine how different the soul-constitution in Europe must have been which, over large areas, inclined people to undertake the Crusades to Asia, to the Orient; especially when one bears in mind how impossible an event like this, resting as it did on an idealistic spiritual background, has become since the beginning of the fifteenth century. People do not consider the completely different nature of humanity's interests before this historical turning-point, nor the interests which, since that time, have become particularly important. But if, from the many characteristics which can be attributed to this more recent time, one wishes to single out the most significant one, then this must be the increasing ascendancy, the increasing intensity of the human power of intellect.

But in the depths of the human soul there is always another force, whether as a sense of longing or as a more or less clear facet of consciousness. It is the longing for knowledge. Now, when one looks back into former times, even into the eleventh, twelfth, thirteenth and fourteenth centuries of European development, it is possible to speak of a definite longing for knowledge in as much as the human being at that time had faculties in his soul which enabled him to achieve a relationship to nature – a relationship to what was revealed in nature as spirit – and thereby also to achieve a relationship to the spirit world itself. Certainly, longing for knowledge has been spoken about a good deal since then; but it is impossible, when one looks completely without prejudice at the development of humanity, to compare the longing for knowledge which holds sway today with the intensity of the longing for knowledge that held sway before the middle of the fifteenth century. Striving for knowledge was an intense affair of the human soul; for knowledge that had an inner glow, an inner warmth, for the human being, and which was also significant for the human being when it came to what moved him to perform his work in the world, and so on. Everything that lived there as a longing for knowledge has become less and less comparable with what has been emerging since the middle of the fifteenth century. And even when we consider the great philosophers of the first half of the nineteenth century, we are presented with ingenious elaborations of the human system of ideas; but only, if I can put it so, artistic elaborations of it. In neither Fichte, nor Schelling, nor Hegel – particularly not in Hegel – do we find a proper idea of what had previously existed as a longing for knowledge.

Then, in the second half of the nineteenth century, the striving for knowledge, even though pursued in isolation as was still the custom, enters more and more into the service of outer life. It enters into the service of technological science and thus also takes on the configuration of this technology. What then is the cause of this? It comes from the fact that it is just in this time that we find the particular development and elaboration of the intellect. This, of course, did not happen all at once. The intellect was gradually prepared for. The last traces of the old clairvoyance had long since become extremely dim. But one can nevertheless say that, to a certain degree, the last effects of the old clairvoyance – though not the old clairvoyance itself – were still present even in the fifteenth century. All human beings, or at least those who strove for knowledge, had some idea of the faculties rising up out of the human soul that are higher than the faculties concerned with daily life. Although in olden times these faculties arose from the soul in a dreamlike way, they were nevertheless faculties different from those of everyday life and it was by means of these other [higher] faculties that people tried to probe to the depths of the world-being – and *did*, in fact, penetrate to its spirituality. Thus was knowledge attained. People experienced it as knowing when, from the phenomena of nature, from the being of nature, they sensed, they perceived, how spiritual elemental beings worked in the individual phenomena of nature; how the divine spiritual being as a whole worked through the totality of nature. People felt themselves to be in the realm of knowledge when gods spoke through the phenomena of nature; when gods spoke through the appearance and movements of the stars. This is what people understood as knowledge.

The moment humanity renounced perception of the spiritual in the manifestations of nature, the concept of knowledge itself also fell more or less into a deterioration. And it is this decline of real intensity in the pursuit of knowledge that marks the latest period of human evolution.

What then is needed here? It is that which exists at present only in the small circle of anthroposophically-striving human beings but which must become more and more general. Nature's manifestations spoke to ancient human beings in such a way that they revealed the spirit to them. The spiritual spoke out of every spring, every cloud, every plant. In the way people came to know the manifestations and beings of nature they also came to know the spiritual. This is no longer the case. But the condition of intellectualism is only a transitional condition. For what is the deepest characteristic of this intellect? It is that it is impossible to grasp and know anything at all with the pure intellect. The intellect is not just there for knowing. This is the greatest error to which the human being can give himself: the belief that the intellect is there for gaining knowledge. People will attain to true knowledge again only when they concern themselves with what lies at the basis of spiritual-scientific research; which, at the least, can be given by Imagination. People will only know truly again when they say: In ancient times divine-spiritual beings spoke from the manifestations of nature. For the intellect they are silent. For higher, supersensible knowledge it will not be the phenomena of nature that will speak directly – for nature, as such, works silently. But beings will speak to the human being – beings who will appear to him in Imaginations, will inspire him, with whom he will become united intuitively and whom he will then be able to relate again to the phenomena of nature. Thus one can say: In ancient times the spiritual appeared to the human being through nature. In our transitional condition we have the intellect. Nature remains spiritless. The human being will lift himself up to a condition where he can again truly know; where, indeed, nature will no longer speak to him of divine-spiritual beings but where he will take hold of the divine-spiritual in supersensible knowledge and will, in turn, be able to relate this to nature.

It was a particular characteristic of oriental spiritual life, of oriental knowledge – which, as we know, lived on as a heritage in occidental civilization – that the orientals, at the time of the blossoming of the knowledge of their culture, perceived a spiritual element in all the manifestations of nature; that the divine-spiritual spoke through nature, whether through the lower elemental beings in individual things and phenomena or in the whole of nature, as the all-encompassing divine-spiritual. Later on there developed in the central regions of the earth that which came under the dialectical-legal spirit. It is out of this that intellectuality was born. Spiritual culture was retained as a heritage from the ancient Orient. And when people still had this last longing to experience something from the Orient – people did experience something of this in the Crusades and brought it back to Europe – and after they had stilled this longing through the Crusades, the Orient became effectively closed off. On the one hand, by what was established by Peter the Great who destroyed the remains of the oriental constitution of soul on the European side and, on the other hand, by the blockade set up by the Turks who, just at the beginning of this age which we call the fifth post-Atlantean epoch, established their rule in Europe. European thought and culture was, as it were, closed off from access to the Orient. But it had to develop further and could only do so under the influence of the dialectical-legal life, under the influence of the economic life arising from the West, and in the decadent continuation of the spiritual life which had been received from the Orient, to which the doors were now closed as I described. The condition was thereby prepared in which we are now living, where it is up to us, out of ourselves, to open the doors again to the spiritual world; to come to a perception of it through Imagination, Inspiration, Intuition.

This is all connected with the fact that, in those ancient times in which the oriental rose to the attainment of wisdom, what was of particular importance were the abilities, the forces, brought by the human being into physical existence through birth. In the time of oriental wisdom, everything – despite the civilization which took its course there and was shone through with wisdom – everything, fundamentally, depended on the blood. But, at the same time, what was in the blood was also spiritually recognized. It was determined by the Mysteries as to who, through his line of blood, was called by destiny to the leadership of the people. There could be no questioning this: whoever was called to the leadership of the people by the Mysteries was brought to this position because his blood-line, his descent, was the outer sign that this was how it should be. There could be no question of any kind of legal proof as to whether anyone was rightly in this position or not because, against the verdict of the gods, according to which people were alloted their place, there could be no contradiction. Jurisprudence was unknown in the Orient. One knew theocracy, the 'rule of cosmic order'. One's mission here in the world of the senses was given by the spiritual world above. The feeling that said that someone was in the right place because the gods had directed his blood-line in such a way that he could be brought to this place was replaced with another in a dialectical-legal dress, on the basis of which one could dispute on legal grounds whether someone was entitled to his position, or to do this or that, and so on.

The nature of the soul-constitution, prepared already in Greece but then particularly also in Rome, by which Central Europeans were beginning to use concepts, dialectics, to decide what justice was, was quite unknown and alien to the Orient. I have described this from different aspects. In the Orient it was a matter of fathoming the will of the gods. And there were no dialectics for deciding what the gods willed.

But we are again at a turning-point. It is becoming necessary now for humanity to also take a closer look at this dialectical-legal element. For the economic element, which from the West has conquered the world with the aid of technology, is already completely entangled in the state of affairs that has arisen through the dialectical-legal aspect. The economy was a minor element in the ancient theocratic cultures which were permeated by the divine-spiritual. People did there in the economic life what arose as a matter of course according to the place and rank into which the gods had placed them through the proclamations of the Mysteries. And then the economic life, which began again only primitively, became caught up, as it were, in the threads of the dialectical-legal life. For, at the beginning of the so-called Middle Ages, the Romans above all had no money. Economics based on money was gradually lost and the dialectical-legal culture spread in Europe as a kind of economy based on nature-produce. The early part of the Middle Ages was, basically, short of money; and this brought about all those forms of military service which were necessary because there was no money to pay the troops. The Romans paid their troops with money. In the Middle Ages feudalism developed, and with it a particular type of professional soldiery. All this came about because, tied to the soil under the influence of an economy based on the exchange of nature-produce, a man could no longer take part himself in distant campaigns of war. Thus this dialectical-legal element grew up in a kind of agricultural economy based on barter, and it was only when technology from the West permeated this economic life that the new age arose. The life of this new civilization, which has become so fragile, has arisen in the fifth post-Atlantean epoch entirely as a result of technology. I have already described this in different ways. I have described how, according to the official census, world population at the end of the nineteenth century was 1,400 million but that as much work was being accomplished as though there were 2,000 million. This is because such a phenomenally large amount of work is done by machines. The machine technology with its stupendous transformation of the economic life and the social life has arrived.

What has not yet arrived — because everything is still engulfed in the intellectual life — is precisely what must now carry this machine-technological economy into modern civilization. One experiences the strangest things today with regard to the prospects facing humanity. There are already many people today, particularly among those who pride themselves on being practical, who, for example, go into governmental positions with their practical experience where it then usually evaporates. The little practical experience people have usually evaporates as soon as they take it into a government department. Such 'governing practicians', such 'practical men in government' – one has to put it in inverted commas – get the strangest ideas these days. Someone said to me recently: 'Yes, the new age has brought us machines, and with them urban life; we must take life back to the land.' As though one could just remove the machine-age from the world! The machine would simply follow us into the country, I said to him. Everything, I said, could be forgotten; spiritual culture could be forgotten, but machines would remain. They would simply be taken out to the land. What has arisen in the cities will transplant itself into the country.

In fact, people become reactionaries in a grand style when they no longer feel inclined – and this is the characteristic of people generally today: that they have no will – to form ideas concerning true progress. They would prefer to bring back the old conditions of the countryside. They imagine that this can be done. They believe that one can shut out what the centuries have brought. That is nonsense! But people today love this nonsense so tremendously because they are too complacent to grasp the new and prefer to get along with the old. The machine age has arrived. Machines themselves show how much human labour they save. It is simply that 500 million people would have to do the work machines do if their work on the earth were to be done by people.

And all this work by machines began, primarily, in Western civilization. It arose in the West and spread to the Orient very late where it did not establish itself at all in the same way as it did in occidental civilization. But that is a time of transition. And now try and grasp a thought which, however strange it may seem to you, must be taken seriously.

Let us suppose the human being in ancient times had before him a cloud, or perhaps a river, or all kinds of vegetation and so on. He did not see in these the dead nature seen by the human being of today – he saw spiritual elemental beings, up to the divine-spiritual beings of the higher Hierarchies. He saw all this, as it were, through nature. But nature no longer speaks of these divine-spiritual beings. We have to grasp them as spiritual reality beyond nature and then relate them again back to nature. The period of transition came. Man created machines as an addition to nature. These he regards for the time being quite abstractly. He works with them in an entirely abstract way. He has his mathematics, geometry, mechanics. With these he constructs his machines and regards them altogether in the abstract. But he will very soon make a certain discovery. Strange though it may still seem to the human being of the present that such a discovery will be made, people will nevertheless discover that (in this mechanistic element which they have incorporated into the economic life) those spirits are again working which in earlier times were perceived by the human being in nature. In his technical machines of the economic sphere the human being will perceive that, although *he* constructed and made them, they nevertheless gradually take on a life of their own – a life certainly which he can still deny because they manifest themselves to begin with only in the economic sphere. But he will notice more and more in what he himself creates that it gains a life of its own and that, despite the fact that he brought it forth from the intellect, the intellect itself can no longer comprehend it. Perhaps people today can barely form a clear idea of this, but it will be so nevertheless. People will discover, in fact, how the objects of their industry (*Wirtschaft*) become the bearers of demons.

Let us look at it from another side. Out of the naked intellect, out of the most desolate intellect, there has arisen the Lenin-Trotsky system that is trying to build an economic life in Russia. Despite Lunacharsky,[2] these people are not interested in the spiritual life. For them the spiritual life must be an ideology arising from the economic life. It can hardly be said that there is a very strong dialectical-legal element in the Trotsky-Leninist system – everything is to be geared towards the economic. The desire is, in a certain sense, to embody the intellect in the economic life. If one could do this for a time – this initial experiment will not work, but let us suppose that it were possible – the economic life would grow over peoples' heads. It would bring forth everywhere destructive, demonic forces out of itself. It would not work because the intellect would not be able to cope with all the economic demands that would surge up! Just as the human being in ancient times beheld nature and the manifestations of nature and saw in them demonic beings; so, too, must the human being of present times learn to see demonic beings in what he himself produces in the economic life. For the time being these demons, which human beings have not diverted into machines, are still in human beings themselves and manifest as the destructive beings (*die zerstörenden*) in social revolutions. These destructive social revolutions are nothing other than the result of not recognizing the demonic element in our economic life. Elemental spirits (*elementarische Geistigkeit*) must be looked for in the economic life just as in ancient times elemental beings (*elementarische Geistigkeit*) were sought in nature. And the purely intellectual life is only an intermediary stage which has no significance at all for nature or for what man produces, but only for human beings themselves.

Human beings have developed the intellect so that they can become free. They have to develop a faculty that has absolutely nothing to do with nature or with machines but only with the human being himself. When the human being develops faculties that stand in a relationship to nature, he is not free. If he tries to flee into the economic life he is also not free because the machines only overwhelm him. But when he develops faculties that have nothing to do with either knowledge or practical life, like pure intelligence, he can appropriate freedom to himself in the course of cultural development. It is precisely through a faculty like the intellect, which does not stand in a relationship to the world, that freedom can arise. But in order that the human being does not tear away from nature, in order that he can again work into nature, Imagination must be added to this intellect; everything must be added to it which supersensible research is seeking to find.

There is something else involved here. I related how, for the ancient oriental, the relationships of the blood line were of very particular importance, for the wise men of the Mysteries were guided by these as though by signs from the gods when they placed the human being into his appropriate [social] position. And all these things reach over then like after-effects, like ghosts, into later times. Then came the dialectical-legal element. The official stamp became the most important thing. The diploma, examination results or, rather, what was on the piece of paper that was the examination certificate – this became the important thing. Whereas in ancient theocratic times blood was the decisive factor, it was now the piece of paper. Those times drew near for which many things are characteristic. A lawyer once said to me during a discussion I had with him: 'The fact that you were born, that you exist, is not what matters!' This did not interest him. It was the birth certificate or the christening certificate that had to exist; that was the important thing. The paper substitute! So the dialectical-legal arose. This, at the same time, is also the expression for the unreal (*das Scheinhafte*) in relation to the world, for the unreal element of the intellect. But precisely in the human being himself there could develop, as the counterpart of this maya element (*Scheinhafte*) in the world, what gave the human being freedom.

But now there develops, out of what is signified in paper – which in earlier times was signified in the blood – out of what is signified in the letter-patent of nobility or similar documents, something that is already showing itself today and which will continue if things go on as now. And they will continue! Descent by blood will no longer be of importance. The letter-patent of nobility and similar papers will have no more importance. At most, only what a man manages to salvage of what he possesses from the past will count. To ask 'why' was not possible when the gods still determined an individual's place in the world. In the dialectical-legal age it was possible to dispute this 'why'. Now all discussion ceases, for only the factual is left, the actuality of what an individual has salvaged. The moment people lose faith in the paper-regime there will be no more discussions. The things an individual has saved for himself will simply be taken away. There is no other way to bring humanity forward, now that nature no longer reveals the spiritual, than to turn to the spiritual itself and, on the other hand, to find in the economic element what people in earlier times found in nature.

This, however, can only be found through association. What a human being alone can no longer find can be found by an association which will again develop a kind of group-soul, taking in hand what the individual at present cannot decide alone. In the Middle Ages, in the age of the intellect, it was the individual that ruled in economics. In the future it will be the association. And people must stand together in an association. And then, when it is recognized that a spiritual element has to be kept in check in the economic life, something will be able to arise which can replace the blood-line and the patent. For, the economic life would grow above the human being's head if he did not show himself equal to it, if he did not bring a spiritual insight with him to guide it. No one would associate with someone who did not bring qualities that made him effective in the economic life and which qualified him really to control the spirits which assert themselves in the economic life. An entirely new spirit will arise. And why will this be so?

In the ancient times, in which people judged according to the blood, what had taken place before birth or before conception was of importance for human beings, for this is what they brought into the physical world through the blood. And when existence before birth had been forgotten a recognition of the life before birth still lived on in the recognition of the blood-line. And then came the dialectical-legal element. The human being was only recognized in relation to what he was as a physical being. Now the other element comes in – an economic life that is growing demonic. And the human being must also now be recognized again in his inmost soul-and-spirit being. And just as one will see the demonic element in economic life, so one will also have to begin to see that which the human being bears through repeated lives on earth. One will have to be aware of what a human being brings when he enters this life. This will have to be taken care of in the spiritual limb of the social organism.

When one judges according to the blood, one really does not need a pedagogy; one only needs a knowledge of the symbols through which the gods express where it is a human being is to be placed. As long as one judges in a purely dialectical-legal way one only needs an abstract pedagogy which speaks of the human child in a generalized way. But when a human being is to be placed in an associative life in such a way that he is fit and capable one has to take account of the following. One must realize that the first seven years in which the human being develops the physical body, are not significant for what he will be able to do later in the social life – he must only be made fit and capable in a general way valid for all human beings. In the years between seven and fourteen, in which the etheric body is developed, the human being must first of all be recognized. What has to be recognized is what then emerges as the astral body at the age of fourteen or fifteen and which comes into consideration when the real soul-and-spiritual core of the human being is to bring him to the place he is meant to be. Here the educational factor becomes a specifically social one. It is a matter here of gaining a true understanding of the child one is educating so that one can see that a certain quality in the child is good for this, and another quality is good for that. But this does not show itself clearly until after the child leaves primary school and it will belong to an artistic pedagogy and didactics to be able to discern that one child is suited for this and another is suited for that. It is according to this that those decisions will be made that are the challenge in *Towards Social Renewal* for the circulation of capital; that is to say the means of production. A completely new spiritual concept must arise which, on the one hand, is capable of perceiving the economic life in its inner spiritual vitality and, on the other, can perceive what role must be played by cultural life; how cultural life must give economic life its configuration. This can only happen if the cultural life is independent, when nothing is forced upon it by the economic life. It is when one inwardly grasps the whole course of humanity's evolution that one recognizes how this evolution requires the threefolding of the social organism.

Thus, because we have been closed off from the Orient in more recent times by the Petrinism of Peter the Great on the one hand and Turkey on the other, we therefore need an independent spiritual life; a spiritual life that really recognizes the spiritual world in a new form and not in the way in which, in ancient times, nature spoke to man. One will then be able to relate this spiritual life back to nature. But once one has found it, one will also be able to develop this spiritual life in such a way in the human being that it becomes the content of his skills; that he will be able through this spiritual life to satisfy, in associative co-operation, an economic life that becomes more and more dynamic. Such thoughts as these really must exist in an anthroposophically-oriented spiritual science. For this reason such a spiritual science can only be born from a knowledge of the course of human evolution.

The first thing is to steer towards a real knowledge of the spirit. Talk of the spirit in general terms – in empty, abstract words in the way that is accepted practice today among official philosophers and in other circles and which has become generally popular – is of no use for the future. The spiritual world is not the same as the physical world. Thus it is not possible to gain a perception of the spiritual world by abstracting from the physical but only by direct spiritual investigation. These perceptions naturally then appear as something completely different from what the human being can know when he knows only the physical world. People who, out of complacency, wish only to know of the physical world call it fantastic to talk about Old Moon, Old Sun and Old Saturn. They find that, when one speaks about these former embodiments of the earth, it strikes no chord in them. Things are described there of which they do not have the foggiest notion. The fact is of course that they have no notion of them because they do not want to know about the spiritual world. Things are related to them about the spiritual world and they say: But it doesn't concur with anything we already know. But that is the whole point: worlds are found that do not concur with what one knows already. This is the way, is it not, that, for example, Arthur Drews, the philosophy professor, judges spiritual science. It does not concur with what he has already imagined. Indeed, when the railway from Berlin to Potsdam was to be built, the post master of Berlin[3] said: And now I'm supposed to send trains to Potsdam! I already send four post coaches a week and no one travels in them. If people really want to throw their money out of the window why don't they do it directly! Of course, the railways looked different from the post-coaches of the 1830s of the honest post-master of Berlin. But, of course, the descriptions of the spiritual world also look different from what nests in heads like Arthur Drews'. He, however, is only characteristic of many others. He is even one of the better ones, strange as it may seem. Not because he is good, but because the others are worse.

It was first of all necessary to show how, on a strict scientific basis, one can truly penetrate into the spiritual worlds. This is what, in the first place, our lecture course this autumn has been striving towards. And even if this is only at its beginnings, it has at least been shown how, in certain areas of the sciences, knowledge can be raised to a knowledge of the spiritual as such and how this spiritual element can in turn permeate what is gained by sense-knowledge.

But what can thus be gained in the field of knowledge and what will be achieved in contrast to the accepted knowledge in the schools – for it is in this area that fine beginnings are apparent – would remain incomplete. One could in fact already show how psychology, and, indeed, even mathematics, point towards spiritual realms. But it would only be something incomplete and therefore unable to aid our declining civilization if a truly elemental and intensive will does not arise from the area of practical economic life. It is necessary that old usages, old habits, be truly dropped and that everyday life be permeated with spirituality. It must come about as a flower of the Anthroposophical Movement that, with the help of the mood of soul that can arise out of spiritual science, a perceptive understanding of practical life is brought to bear – especially of the practical economic life – and that it may be shown how the downfall can be averted if a consciousness of creating something alive is carried into this economic life.

Every day one should keep an ever-watchful eye on the so blatantly visible signs of our declining economic life. This old economic life cannot be galvanized. For just as today no one should be proud of what he gains from ordinary science – for that would definitely lead humanity into the future prophesied by Oswald Spengler – so, too, no one should be proud of what he can gain from the old economic life by way of abilities that correspond to this old form. Today no one can be proud of being a physicist, a mathematician, a biologist in the usual sense. But also no one can be proud of being a merchant, an industrialist in the old sense. But this 'old sense' is the only thing we have today. Nowhere today do we see anything arising like a true association. What is really needed, as a kind of second event of this Goetheanum, is to have something on the lines of this lecture-course, which could provide something tangible out of the realm of practical life itself, and which could stand side by side with the sciences. We will not get any further with what is contained in just one stream but only when this other side of human striving also has its place.

This today is still the characteristic feature of our present human evolution: on the one side the traditional bearers of the old spiritual life who calumniate and slander one when, working out of the modern scientific approach, one tries to achieve a spiritualization. They already do this today quite consciously because they have no interest in the progress of human development and because, for the time being, they only think to hold back this evolution of humanity. Sometimes they do so in a truly grotesque manner, like that strange academic[4] who recently spoke in Zürich about Anthroposophy and went to such extremes that even his colleagues were shocked; so that, as it seems, this attack against Anthroposophy has actually acted as mild propaganda for it. These representatives of a redundant spiritual life persist, however, and will do so far more, for they will close ranks with formidable slanders. Here one sees what one is up against, arising in the form of slanders and so on, in regard to untruth.

On the other side one can notice another strong resistance; which, however, occurs in the unconscious. And this is a painful experience. In this area one can definitely speak of an inner opposition, sometimes quite unintentional, against what must lie in the direction of spiritual-scientific endeavour. It will be a matter of having to learn, particularly in this area, to identify with the aims that spiritual science can set here. For to judge, in the subjective way that has been usual up to now, what must be willed from spiritual science, would be to do the same as the priests and others in other areas do when they declare spiritual science a heresy. This is what makes difficulties for our Anthroposophical Movement – the fact that precisely in this area a kind of inner opposition is clearly noticeable. One can say that it is particularly in this area that what sheds light in such a strange way on certain accusations which come from many sides, shows itself most clearly. They say: 'In this Anthroposophical Society everyone only repeats what one man has said. But in reality they do not repeat at all; everyone just says what he thinks so that the one man can approve it.' We have experienced this many times, have we not? A person talks frequently about what he may want, saying that I said so, even though from me he actually heard the exact opposite. Now this is the real rule of blind faith in authority. A strange faith in authority! This has been evident in many cases. But it would be particularly damaging if this strange kind of opposition – there has actually always been more opposition than faith in authority and, therefore, an indictment of faith in authority is really unjust – it would be far more fatal if what I refer to here as inner opposition were, particularly in the sphere of practical life, to take on wider dimensions. For then the opponents of anthroposophical striving would, as long as they could, of course say: 'Aha, a sectarian, fantastic movement which cannot be practical.' Of course it cannot be practical if people do not engage themselves in it; just as, after all, no matter how good one is at sewing, one cannot sew without a needle.

With this I only wished to draw attention to something that needs watching. It is by no means intended as a criticism or as a reference to the past but is something necessary for the future. Nevertheless, I would of course not have referred to it if I did not see all sorts of smoke-clouds rising. But I am really only pointing out what has, as it were, to be a challenge to really co-operate on all sides and not to shelter behind reactionary practices and, behind the bulwark of these reactionary practices, destroy Anthroposophy even though one is perhaps trying to help it. So I am not referring to something that has already happened but to something that is necessary for the future. It is necessary to think about these things.

With these comments I shall have to let it rest for today. Tomorrow and the following day we shall have to link up this prelude which, as you will see, is in fact an introduction to a study of the Christ-experience in the twentieth century.

Dornach, 30 October 1920

If an understanding for what one can call the reappearance of Christ is to find its place in the soul in the right way it is necessary to create a preparatory understanding for the course that the Christ-idea, the image people have had of the Christ, has taken in the course of human development. We remember that human development has proceeded from a constitution of soul which we have often called a kind of instinctive perception; a clairvoyance which was dim and dreamlike. And we have, on repeated occasions, characterized the different epochs of human development in such a way that we have placed the corresponding form of this constitution of soul into different times.

Today we will remind ourselves that there were still strong remnants of this old clairvoyant condition of humanity existing at the time of the occurrence of the Mystery of Golgotha. The Mystery of Golgotha is to be understood in the first place as a *fact*, but as a fact which, in its inner essence, can never be grasped by the intellect which since the middle of the fifteenth century has constituted the soul-life of modern civilization but which was already prepared for in Greek and Roman times. Thus one can say: During the course of Greek and Roman history, when the Mystery of Golgotha was accomplished on the earth, there were still strong remnants of the ancient clairvoyance existing in many people. Other people had already lost this clairvoyance – were already definitely in the beginnings of an intellectual development. This was particularly so in the Romans. And one can therefore say that, in its reality, in its essence, the Mystery of Golgotha was grasped at first only by those who still had a remnant of the old clairvoyance. It could be described – the symbolism too could be indicated – by those who had these remnants. This instinctive clairvoyance was a particular characteristic of the ancient oriental peoples and existed essentially in its last remnants above all in these peoples.

And Christ Jesus, too, did, after all, walk on the earth among oriental people.

Thus the Mystery of Golgotha was understood first of all through the remnants of ancient oriental wisdom. And when this Mystery of Golgotha moved towards the West – to the Greeks and the Romans – one could receive what was related by those people who, out of the remains of the old clairvoyance, had understood what had really come to pass on the earth. And in order that there could be a perception through an 'eye-witness' of the soul there arose in St Paul, through a particular enlightenment which came to him at a late period of his life, a clairvoyant state through which he could convince himself of the truth, of the genuine nature, of the Mystery of Golgotha. What St Paul was able to relate out of his conviction – what those who had preserved the remains of an old clairvoyance could bring forward concerning the Mystery of Golgotha out of an ancient oriental wisdom, could be received by people as news – could be clothed in the form of the germinating intellect. Intellect itself, however, was not able to penetrate the Mystery of Golgotha.

The way in which those who still had remains of the old clairvoyance spoke about the Mystery of Golgotha is called Gnosis. And, if I can put it so, the form of speaking about the Mystery of Golgotha in the way that was possible with these remnants of old clairvoyance – this was Christian Gnosis. And the presentation of the Mystery of Golgotha then reached posterity in the way I have described in my book *Christianity as Mystical Fact*. Thus the first understanding of the Mystery of Golgotha was attained through these remains of the old clairvoyance; through the ancient, instinctive oriental perception. One could say that this ancient oriental perception was preserved up to the Mystery of Golgotha to such a degree that a truly human grasp of this Mystery could find a place before the intellect broke in and understanding for the Mystery of Golgotha could no longer be found. Had the Mystery of Golgotha come during the full flowering of the intellect it would, of course, have made no impression on humanity at all.

Thus the tidings of the Mystery of Golgotha lived in the accounts of the old clairvoyants and, basically, as you know from my *Christianity as Mystical Fact*, the Gospels are nothing other than accounts concerning the Mystery of Golgotha gained through clairvoyance. But then there spread out over humanity's development the wave which had already taken root in Greece, as I have described to you, which had its source particularly in Rome and which can be seen as the wave that prepared the later intellectuality but in which this intellectuality already lived. Dialectical-legal thinking spread out and, in turn, led to civic-political thinking. This spread from the South into those northern regions where, as I related yesterday, there was still a nature-based economy. Central European civilization, nourished at first by Rome, took shape primarily in the sign of the intellectual, the dialectical-legal, development of the human soul. In the midst of everything that occurred here people could no longer themselves behold the Mystery in the sense of the old spirituality, but received the accounts, the traditions, and clothed these in the forms of their own soul-constitution. People clothed it more and more in dialectics. Through Rome the Mystery of Golgotha became clothed in dialectics. Out of what was Christian Gnosis, which still relied on vision, there took shape the pure dialectical theology which went hand in hand with the establishing of the European Empire that later became [nation] States. But the first great Empire was actually the secularized ecclesiastical 'Empire of the Church', permeated by Roman judicial forms. Many external facts show how this dialectical-legal, political thinking, in which the old oriental direct perception clothed itself, spread out over Europe.

Charlemagne, for example, was a vassal of the Pope who had bestowed on him his title of Emperor. And when one studies the whole extent of the rulership of Charlemagne, one finds among the forces through which his rulership spread an ecclesiastical-theological influence. It was a kind of theocratic empire that spread there but it was everywhere permeated by dialectical-legal forms. The clergy were the bureaucracy. They held the offices of the State and united in their person the political and ecclesiastical elements. The old spiritual life based on spiritual vision – which, as you know, had abolished the spirit in 869 – this old spiritual life moves over entirely into a political Church-Empire which extends over the greater part of Europe.

You know from history and from what I have related here from the spiritual-scientific point of view how this continuous cross-flow of the Roman ecclesiastical element, and that which tried more or less to free itself from it, produced conflicts, and how these conflicts really form a great part of medieval history. But one must look at the immense difference that exists between the whole social structure of the Middle Ages, which then dissolved into the modern states, and the social structure of the ancient Orient which was entirely permeated by the spirit, by the old instinctive clairvoyance, and all that this brought with it.

From what source did this ancient oriental vision receive its content? It was – one cannot put it differently – 'inborn' (*Angeborensein*); for the sages of the Mysteries sought as their pupils those who had inborn faculties of such a nature that they were able to come to this instinctive perception. Out of the great mass of people those were chosen in whose blood it lay to have such vision. Thus one simply knew that in the human beings that were sent as children from the spiritual worlds into this physical world came remnants of the experiences in those spiritual worlds. (I am still speaking of the time in which the Mystery of Golgotha approached or was already accomplished.) In one individual these came less; in another, more. With the blood, so to say, echoes from the experiences in the spiritual worlds came in. Those who had the largest number of instinctive memories of experiences before birth or conception were the suitable pupils for the Mysteries. They were able to comprehend and see, or, rather, were able through comprehending vision to recognize the intentions of the gods regarding human beings, for they had experienced this before birth and had an instinctive memory of it in this life on earth. And they were sought out by the wise men of the Mysteries, by the priests, to be placed before humanity as individuals who could bear witness to the will of the spiritual world with regard to the physical world. It was human beings such as these who were the first ones able to speak about the Mystery of Golgotha. One can certainly say that this was a very different way of placing a human being in the social order. He was placed in this social order by the gods themselves through the recognizing of this fact by the Mysteries.

The inborn faculties based on the action of the blood then gave way to the medieval wave. Human beings then had nothing, or they had less and less, of what is brought into the physical world at birth from the spiritual worlds. Certainly the people who counted had nothing of this. Nothing but an instinctive memory remained. So upon what basis could a social structure be founded? What could this be founded on in the dialectical-legal age? It could only be founded on authority – the authority claimed above all by the Popes of Rome. It was this authority that took the place of that which the priests of the ancient Mysteries had beheld and recognized as being sent from the spiritual worlds. In ancient times decisions were made as to what should happen in the social life according to what was brought from the spiritual worlds. This could now only be decided in that certain people – that is the Roman Popes and, by extension, the individual vassal princes of the Popes, the kings and other princes – were ascribed with a certain authority on earth, and ascribed through legal justification, by formal, legal right. Men must now command, since the gods no longer commanded. And who was to command had now to be established through external law.

Thus arose the medieval principle of authority and one can say that into this principle was also incorporated the whole perception of the Mystery of Golgotha which one only received as an account. At most one could clothe it in symbols, in which, however, one only had images. A symbol of this kind is the mass with the sacred Last Supper and all that the Christian could experience in the Church. In the Last Supper he had directly present, according to his comprehension, the entry of the Christ-force into the world. The fact that this Christ-force was able to stream into the physical world for the believers was subject to the authority which in turn proceeded from the ordinations of the Roman Church.

But what was developing here as the dialectical-legal Roman element also bore in its bosom, as it were, its other side. It bore the continuous protest against authority. For when everything is based on authority, as was the case in the Middle Ages, then there also already comes to expression in the human being that which is to come in the future: inner protest *against* authority. This inner protest against authority came to light through the most diverse historical phenomena, through such people as Wyclif,[1] Hus[2] and so on, who set themselves against the bare principle of authority, who wished to comprehend Christ out of their inner being – for which, however, the time had not yet come. In fact, one could only give onself up to the illusion that one grasped Christ out of one's own inner being.

Those men who still made their appearance as mystics in the Middle Ages also spoke of the Christ, but they did not yet have the Christ-experience. But they did have the old accounts concerning the Christ. And this rebellion against authority became stronger and stronger and because of this the urge to fortify this authority also naturally became stronger and stronger. And the strongest exercise of power to fortify this authority – to put, in a sense, everything that proceeds from the Mystery of Golgotha only on a basis of authority and permanently so – came from Jesuitism. Jesuitism has nothing more of the Christ. Jesuitism already contains in itself a complete rebellion against the original understanding of Christ. The first understanding occurred in Gnosis with the remains of the oriental clairvoyance. Jesuitism took up only the intellectual-dialectic element and rejected the Christ-principle. It did not develop a Christology but a fighting doctrine for Jesus: a Jesuology. Even though Jesus was seen as one reaching beyond all human beings, that which led to the Mystery of Golgotha through Jesuitism was nevertheless to be something founded purely on authority.

Thus was prepared the situation which then came about, with its culmination in the nineteenth century, in which the Christ-impulse as something spiritual was completely lost – in which theology, in wishing to be a modern theology, wanted to speak only of the man Jesus. But as this whole development took its course it gave rise to many difficult conditions. Take the fact that the existing accounts concerning the Mystery of Golgotha were taken up by the Roman principle into a purely juristic dialectics; that they were taken up through external symbolism which could be explained. It was then impossible to let these accounts, as they existed, come into the hands of the faithful. Thus the strict forbiddance for those of the Roman faith to read the Bible.

This was the most important fact right into the later Middle Ages; that the faithful were forbidden to read the Bible. It was considered by the priesthood and the leading Catholic circles that it would be the most frightful thing if the Gospels were to become known among the broad mass of the faithful. For the Gospels originate out of a completely different constitution of soul. The Gospels can only be understood through a spiritual constitution of soul. A dialectical soul-constitution can make nothing of them. It was therefore impossible for those times, in which the intellect and dialectics were prepared, to allow the masses access to the Gospels. The Church fought furiously against the Gospels becoming known and regarded those who went against the prohibition of reading them as the most flagrant heretics; like, for example, the Waldenses and Albigenses. These claimed the right to teach themselves about the Mystery of Golgotha through the Gospels. The Church opposed this because it knew full well that the way the Church itself presented the Mystery of Golgotha was irreconcilable with a common knowledge of the Gospels. For the Gospel in its true form actually consists of four Gospels which contradict one another. They knew that if they gave out the Gospels to the great mass of the faithful, the faithful would straightaway be confronted with contradictory accounts which, with the dawning intellectuality, they could only grasp as something to be understood as one understands things of the physical plane. After all, with an event on the physical plane one cannot understand why it ought to be described in four different ways. For an event that has to be understood by higher forces one is concerned with how it looks from this or that view, since it must always be seen from different sides. I have often said that this holds true even for dreams. People can dream the same thing; that is to say the same thing can take place within them but the pictures that are formed can differ in the most manifold ways. Thus for someone who stands in a spiritual relation to the Mystery of Golgotha the contradictions are of no significance.

But the people at the dawn of the Middle Ages did not stand in a spiritual relation; they stood in the sign of dialectics right into the lowest classes of the people. And for dialectics one could not simply give out a fourfold mutually contradictory account of the Mystery of Golgotha. And when Protestantism emerged and the Church could no longer maintain the prohibition of the Bible, there arose that discrepancy in European life which then led to the modern theology of the nineteenth century which finally erased from the Gospels everything that was contradictory. And what the Gospels have now become is, in the end, really just a well-picked carcass. The most meagre that has appeared, the most plucked, are the things which the famous Schmiedel[3] has discovered. He considers the only genuine places in the Gospels are those where someone is not praised, where something disapproving is said, and dismisses everything else. And thus there arose the descriptions of Jesus of the theologians of the nineteenth and the beginning of the twentieth century, who only wanted to describe Jesus the man and believed that with that they could still remain within Christianity. An intellectual-dialectical age could only remain within Christianity by prohibiting the Gospels. With the Gospels a dialectical-legal age could only have the effect of gradually eliminating the figure of Christ completely.

Modern humanity has actually developed under this untruth. This humanity has absolutely no inkling that, fundamentally, it lives under the principle of authority but continually denies that this is so. There is hardly a stronger stamp of the belief in authority than exists among those who accept modern official science as the standard for the world. Just look how easily people are satisfied when they are told somewhere that something has been 'scientifically proven'. They know nothing more about this proof than that it has been stated by someone who has been to grammar school and university, has become a lecturer or professor and has therefore been appointed again by authority. This is how this is promulgated. And then what gets out among people in this way is supposed to be true science. Just try sometime to hold in mind for yourself everything that people accept nowadays as being true, proven science. In the last analysis it rests upon nothing other than a pure principle of authority, on absolute faith in authority – it is only that people delude themselves about this. This is the belief in authority that has replaced the other way of ordering the social structure which was derived from the Orient.

And one must grasp what hatred developed within those circles who had no understanding at all for the Mystery of Golgotha, who had only tradition continued through authority, and were terrified of the Gospels becoming generally known among the masses. One must grasp the hatred that became ever stronger and stronger and especially in Jesuitism was developed into a complete system – a hatred for Gnosis. And even today we still see how theologians get hot under the collar whenever there is any talk of Gnosis! We have to understand this on the basis of the development of European humanity. One must, for example, understand the development of the universities. How have the universities developed? One should look at history from the eleventh to the fourteenth centuries. They developed out of the Church. The monastery schools have become universities. Everything that was taught had to have the stamp of approval from Rome and only what had received this stamp was to be believed. The thought that it had to be approved by Rome was gradually lost but the thought that it had to be approved by something remained. And thus there remained the principle of authority even in those who no longer believed in Roman authority. And this continuation of the Roman authority-principle, but without a belief in Rome itself, is the mentality of our universities today. It is also the mentality in Protestant countries. The Catholic Church only fights on for its authority, with the exclusion of everything spiritual; it calumniates everything that goes beyond its dialectical-legal mode of thinking, calumniates everything which resists being fitted into the social authority principle. One must only understand how deeply this has penetrated into the soul-constitution of those human beings living at the dawn of our modern civilization. In this way the majority lost the power to face the truth for themselves and in the last resort this has produced the great confusion; the frightful chaos in which we are now living.

But at the same time we are now living in an age in which a faculty of vision, of supersensible perception, is again being prepared. It is the wish of spiritual science to prepare for this faculty which humanity must take hold of again. Not the old instinctive vision, but a supersensible perception founded on full consciousness. Theology professors and others fight against this perception; they confuse it with the old Gnostic visionary gift and say all sorts of things they do not understand themselves against this modern faculty. But this new vision is rising up as a necessity which must take hold of humanity. And it is into this faculty of vision that a true comprehension of the

Mystery of Golgotha can shine again.

Thus, the course of man's image of Christ is as follows. The Mystery of Golgotha takes place at a time in which remnants of the old clairvoyance still exist. Human beings can still just about understand it. They set down this understanding in the Gospels. Christianity moves westwards and it taken up by Rome in the dialectical spirit. It is understood less and less. People talk in words about the Mystery of Golgotha; in words that are merely words so that the faithful are also quite content when they are in church and the priest speaks words in a language they do not understand. For it is not a matter for them of understanding but a matter, at most, of living in the general atmosphere which is directed to the Mystery of Golgotha. And the real connection of human beings with the Mystery of Golgotha is lost. It is lost more and more. At a certain point in the Middle Ages people begin to debate the significance of the symbol in which the continuous communication of the Mystery of Golgotha had clothed itself. People begin to debate, for example, the significance of the Last Supper. But as soon as people begin to debate something it means they no longer understand it. What lives in the evolution of humanity lives as experience; as long as people have the experience they do not dispute it. When the conflict over the nature of the Last Supper arose in the Middle Ages the very last traces of understanding for the Last Supper were gone – the play of dialectics had already taken possession of it. And so the modern life of humanity unfolded until the prohibition of the Bible could no longer hold. In theory, all Catholics are still forbidden to read it. Theoretically they are allowed to read only that extract that is prepared as if the Gospels were a unity. Even today it is strictly forbidden for Catholics to occupy themselves with the four Gospels because, of course, the moment one goes into the four gospels with the modern spirit, where they are read in the same way one reads an account of the physical plane, they fragment into shreds. It is irresponsible when people who are fully aware of this and who have also experienced how in the course of the nineteenth century, under the philologizing of theology, the Gospels have been destroyed – when these people have the cheek, it cannot be called anything else, to say that Anthroposophy explains the Gospels in an arbitrary way, that it reads all sorts of things into them. These people know that the connection with the Mystery of Golgotha is lost if the Gospels are not understood in a spiritual sense. One experiences people getting up onto the platform and again and again gabbling from a Catholic or Protestant point of view about how Anthroposophy puts things into the Gospels although they know perfectly well that if no spiritual comprehension is given to the Gospels they must radically destroy the Christian constitution of soul. If people would only pay more attention to how the majority of those who utter such nonsense about Anthroposophy are really only concerned with keeping their office in the most comfortable way, in the way they learnt in their youth – if people knew that in these theologians there is living not the slightest feeling for truth but only fear of losing their comfortable way of comprehending things – then we would get much further in rejecting the sort of Frohnmeyers[4] and similar people who no longer possess the slightest spark of any sense of truth.

What is to be saved today is the Mystery of Golgotha itself. And preparation must be made so that this Mystery of Golgotha may shine forth again to human imagination. For it cannot shine forth to the intellect. The intellect can only dissolve it. The intellect can either only wipe it from the world with its art of philology or preserve it by a tyrannical authority in the Jesuitical sense which does not strive for truth but only for a comfortable life. For those, however, who strive for truth the path today leads towards Imagination; that is to conscious perception of the spiritual world. And the important thing is that, from the vantage point of this conscious perception of the spiritual world, one should be in the position to comprehend once again the whole being of humanity. Above all, it is essential that all human education and instruction be given from this point of view.

We know that until the age of seven, until the change of teeth, the child lives in imitation. Imitation is, in fact, nothing less than a continuation of what, in a completely different form, was present in the spirit world before birth or conception. There, in the spiritual world, one being merges into another and this is then expressed in the child's imitation of the people around it, as an echo of its spiritual experiences. Then, from the seventh year, from the change of teeth up to puberty, comes the child's need for authority. What still lives in childish imitation lived in a certain way in the whole human nature during the ancient oriental culture. Those who worked out of the Mysteries worked with such a powerful force that other human beings followed them, as the child follows the grown-ups in its environment. Then came the principle of authority. And now the human being is growing out of this principle and is growing into that principle which begins to show itself after puberty – although of course in a personal, individual way, different from the way it is in the development of humanity as a whole. Today the human being is approaching the time when it will be necessary to develop in himself something which cannot be developed of itself. The child comes into the world as an imitator. In the ancient oriental social life it also came into the world as an imitator. But what lived in the child as the principle of imitation remained active even into the time of authority: the time of discerning judgements, remained active with regard to social affairs and everything that was encompassed as the religious life. The authority-principle in the ancient Orient applied only to the immediate environment. The greater affairs of life remained in the form of child-like experience.

These larger affairs of life then came into the times of the Middle Ages. The authority-principle prevailed and now, for the first time, a withdrawl from the authority-principle asserted itself – the principle of individual judgement arose. All that was developed for the affairs of the religious life, the artistic life – for human life in general that goes over and beyond the immediate elementary affairs of nature – could be found in the child, who brought it with him into the physical world from the spiritual worlds through the blood. When the authority-principle still held sway, one only needed to build upon something which, with a certain necessity, developed out of the still quite unconscious etheric body. Today, when the principle of independent judgment is appearing, there arises an enormous new responsibility for pedagogy and didactics. There arises the fact that one must look in the growing child towards what will emerge. When a child reaches the age of fifteen the astral body is born in him. There is born in him that which carries into the world – now not unconsciously but in a more and more conscious way – the experiences of the spiritual world.

The time is approaching when in all our education and training we must look to what emerges from the child when he is in the fourteenth, fifteenth years of life. This was not of such great importance in all earlier times for it is connected with what lives independently in the human being which he does not bring with him through birth and which he cannot receive through authority but must really draw out of himself. And in order that he may draw it out of himself rightly we must take care that the child has the right upbringing and education up to the fourteenth, fifteenth years so that in those years he can then develop the astral body in the right way. Education and training take on a completely new significance in our modern time and, in fact, there should be no more teaching without insight into the relation of the human being to the spiritual world. That is the battle that is arising.

The sense of 'I' which pressed to the surface of human consciousness in the idealistic philosophy of Central Europe asserted itself, as it were, out of still instinctive depths. In Fichte, Schelling, Hegel, however, this sense of 'I' dealt only with what man experiences between birth and death and had nothing to do with what is the super-physical human being. I said yesterday that the Mid-European was cut off by Turkey and by the influence of Peter the Great from anything oriental. But what continued to hover before the Mid-European as a revelation still lived on as an inheritance. This was really only understood out of the clairvoyance of the ancient Orient but still had its echoes in Asiatic Russia, the Russia not yet Europeanized.

Revelation is still alive today in Asia although in a completely decadent form. A sense for revelation is there still. The intellectual, the purely dialectical element, belongs to the West and is only developed today for the economic life. The Mid-European element was always hemmed in between these two – the Western intellectualism, still entirely restricted to the earthly economic, human reason that wishes to occupy itself only with external experience, and the oriental revelation. And the clouds gathered ever more threateningly since only a kind of rhythmic balance existed between revelation and reason. What the great Scholastics of the Middle Ages had sought to hold apart – a rational grasp of the outer sense-world and supersensible revelation – collided increasingly into one another as the modern age arose. And we see this mutual interlocking particularly in the first half of the nineteenth century when the idealistic philosophy of Central Europe was born. We see then how the Western element expands in the second half of the nineteenth century; how, to a certain degree, the whole of Europe, even up to Russia, is Anglicized, and how the crushed condition, the devastated state, of Central Europe is an external sign of a deep inner process which humanity today is unwilling to grasp. Everything that is hemmed in between West and East is razed to the ground, is dashed to pieces, and does not know what to do. It lives in upheavals; talks of all sorts of things by which, somehow or other, progress can be made – but talks, however, nothing but nullities. This is expressed right into small details. There is an utter inability to cope with economics under the old conditions. What do people do? They either squeeze out of the old what is still left by a dreadful tightening of taxation or they fill what is lacking by printing worthless notes; millions of bank-notes a week. And though it is perhaps only a symbol, there nevertheless stands before the soul of individual people the following: a decadent clinging to revelation in the East, the nullity of the Centre and the rationality of the West, still bogged down in economics. And yet they talk as if of a future perspective – as though the Centre were simply not there – of the great conflict that lies ahead between Japan and America.

People, of course, picture this purely physically. This also signifies something of immense profundity. And when the decadent element existing in the East and that which is as yet unborn in the West clash together through ignoring the Centre – then the sense of 'I' which came to expression in the Centre is submerged in that chaos that arises through the crushing from East to West. Contemplation of the 'I' vanished with the idealistic philosophy of Central Europe. It has ceased to exist since the middle of the nineteenth century. And what people tried to create as political structure out of the upheavals – that, too, lies on the ground today. Impossible political structures spring up like that of Czechoslovakia which, quite certainly, in the long run cannot live and cannot die. These impossible structures can only spring up through the fact that peace is made by the people of the West who have no idea what the conditions for life are in the Centre. In Zurich people listen to someone or other who comes from Paris and holds forth to them brilliantly, as one says, on the unity of the Slovak and the Czech elements. The listeners are astounded at what such a professor makes known about the predestination of Czechoslovakia, because they have no idea of the conditions for life in the East and because they do not know that what is brought into being there is only the squeezing element, the crushing together of East and West. People still cover their eyes so as not to see what the external symptoms are saying. You won't believe how, even here in Central Europe, scenes take place – though at the present time still very much towards the East – where remnants of the troops who carried the war on their shoulders appear here and there. They are now officers although there is no justification for this under present conditions. They make innocent women dance naked before them and then thrust bayonets into their bellies. Such scenes actually take place at the command of people who, incidentally, fought bravely in the war.

Before all these things the deluded men of the West, who conclude a peace of which they understand nothing, cover up their eyes. They do not see how, in what is actually going on, significant things proclaim themselves. And, for the most part, people go on with life as though nothing were happening in the world at all. And thus, one could say, things are driven into the very narrowest corner of the consciousness. That which once brought forth such idealistic heights – such ideas as one finds in Goethe, Fichte, Schelling, Hegel – in reality no longer exists in public life. And when it tries to assert itself, as here in the Goetheanum, it is slandered. Trumped-up slanderous stuff crops up everywhere; people cite it as something which they pretend to understand and must pass judgment on. Something is developing into nullity which a century ago was still radiant spirit-life. And above this the clouds are rolling together from the East and the West.

And what is the meaning of this that must come to expression in the most frightful way in coming decades? What is its meaning? On the one hand it is the challenge to stand firm on the ground that would give birth to the new life of the spirit. On the other hand it is the sign in the heavens of that which has been spoken about among us for some time: the approach of the Christ in the form in which He must be seen from the twentieth century onwards. For, before the middle of this century has passed, the Christ must be seen. But before that, all that remains of the old must be driven into nullity, the clouds must gather. The human being must find his full freedom out of nullity and the new perception must be born out of this nullity. The human being must find his whole strength out of the nothingness. It is but the desire of spiritual science to prepare him for it. This is something of which one may not say that it desires to, but that it *must* desire to!

Dornach, 31 October 1920

I tried yesterday to describe to you something of how European conditions are bound to develop in the near future, and we saw that the course of European development, of modern civilisation generally, will inevitably be bound up with the disappearance of what, in many areas of our modern times, is still considered by people to be the easiest way and of value. From the way in which I had to speak yesterday it will be clear to you that, for many who would rather go through the coming times in a comfortable sleep, with a sleeping soul, there is a very disagreeable awakening in store. I do not say – I mentioned this yesterday already – that the prophecies of those who see the most central matter of the near future as lying in such external things as the differences between Japan and America must be absolutely correct. But what must be regarded as imminent is what I characterized for you in a few brush-strokes as the great spiritual battle between East and West, in which the true culture of Middle Europe, as we have come to know it in recent weeks, will be wedged.

Strange as this may sound it is out of the modern world-conception, based on science, that the most intense need will have to arise for what I have called the Christ-experience soon to come.

We learnt yesterday how little experience of the Christ there really is at the present time. The course of human evolution has brought it about that ever since the Mystery of Golgotha, and particularly in recent centuries, all that can properly be called experience of the Christ has fallen into complete decadence. We saw, too, that because of the impossibility of adhering to the old prohibition against reading the Gospels – which, in theory, is indeed still maintained by the Catholic Church against humanity's demand to be able to receive and read the Gospels – an experience of Christ has not been able to develop. And we have already pointed out how the particular constitution of soul that is becoming prevalent in modern civilization will again lead to experience of the Christ, just as remnants of the old instinctive clairvoyance could lead to it at the time of the Mystery of Golgotha. But one has to be clear that just as other crucial, incisive events in human evolution came about in ways other than is expected among philistine circles; so, too, what one must call the Christ-experience of the first half of the twentieth century will come in an unexpected way. And this experience will have a clearly definable connection with the modern outlook on life based on science.

Consider the following. Since the middle of the fifteenth century the constitution of people's souls has become quite different from what it was before that time. History does not take this into account because external history ever and again remains at the surface of things. But especially during the period between the middle of the nineteenth century and our own time, the soul-constitution of humanity as a whole has undergone a fundamental change. This also has been taken into account far too little because people habitually stick to what was once instilled into them. At most, one can notice a breaking out from this clinging by force of habit to what has been inculcated when one observes with a wakeful soul the outlook on life of today's younger generation, and compares this with the outlook of their elders when *they* were in their youth. The difference between older people and the youth of today has been depicted again and again, particularly by poets; and if people did not encapsulate themselves in their habitual ideas so that nothing can penetrate which conflicts with their usual habits of thought they would soon see what an immense gulf there really is between those who are old today and those who are young.

On the other hand there is a terribly reactionary, conservative element in human evolution today. It is the belief in the authority of popular science. And this is connected with the fact that popular science has totally captivated the general consciousness. People underestimate this today. Just think how rapidly, especially in the last decades, ideas which have become familiar through nineteenth-century scientific development have taken universal hold, right down to the least educated classes. Certainly there are many who still cling to a certain piety, a piety that wants to know nothing of what is laying hold of humanity through modern scientific thought. But for the most part there is a terrible dishonesty rooted in this piety; a refusal to face what is spreading here and which one can only define as the materialism of modern humanity evoked by natural science.

The spread of this materialism will not be checked in the near future as some deluded scientists seem to think. On the contrary, it will increase with furious speed and we shall see how, out of the chaos of modern civilization, this materialistic mood will become stronger and stronger. And if sufficient preparation has been made, if the aims of spiritual science are fulfilled – so that children at school are given a stimulus for the right kind of development – then out of this materialistic mood, out of this chaos, individual souls can emerge who will have a very strong sense of something which I should now like to describe, although I have done so in different ways and at different times before.

When someone acquainted with the modern scientific outlook on the world, observes it with awakened eyes of the soul, he cannot fail to realize that one of its most distinguishing features is that it is incapable of comprehending the human being. The human being, as such, is actually entirely excluded from the conception of the world based on modern science. We had occasion here recently to consider the scope of the various branches of scientific learning when we held our course for scientists and we saw that none of these has anything to say about the real nature of man.

We need only give one characteristic example: take the usual theory of evolution expounded under the influence of Darwin or Weismann[1] or others. It demonstrates the evolution of the living creature from the simplest to the most perfect and lays down the view that man also derives his origin from this line of evolution. But actually it takes into consideration only that element of man that is animal. It considers man only so far as to be able to say that any organ, any structure in man, derives from the corresponding organ or structure in the animal line. Science ignores the extent to which the animal-element in man appears in a modified form, the extent to which the animal-nature in man differs from that of the animal world. The ability to keep man himself in view has been completely lost by science; man is left out.

Science has developed scrupulous methods. It has established a certain discipline that is necessary if one means to enter into discussions on world-views. But this science has not been capable of raising man's power of understanding to the point where man himself becomes comprehensible. There is no place for the human being in the scientific thought of today and thus he presents an ever-greater riddle to himself. Only a very few people are aware of this today and these few can certainly be clear about it theoretically. But there is, as yet, no unified feeling for it. Such a feeling will arise with vigour from properly conducted elementary education. The children will come out of properly conducted elementary school in such a way that they will already have the feeling: 'We have a science which is born out of modern intellectuality, but the further we enter into this science, the more we learn of nature, the less we understand of ourselves, the less we understand of the human being.'

This intellect, which was the principal soul-force developing in recent centuries – and is so still today – this intellect creates a complete void in man, so to speak, as regards his perception of self. And yet, on the other hand, we hear the demand that man should stand solely on the basis of his own being. This comes forward as, I should say, a fundamental social demand. Side by side with the inability of the science of recent times to account for the human being, we have, on the other side, claims of all kinds coming not from any scientific impulse but from the depths of human instinct – demands that man be able to raise himself to an existence worthy of the human being: that he should be able to feel what his real nature is. While on the one hand we have more and more demands of a practical kind, on the other we have the increasing inability of science to say anything about the human being's own nature. Such a discrepancy in human experience would have been quite impossible in earlier times of human world-view development.

If we turn once more to the ancient oriental outlook we must say, from what we have been able to indicate of this, that the human being knew then that he descended from spiritual heights; that he lived, before he entered into physical existence through conception and birth, in a spiritual world. He knew that he brought with him from the spiritual world something that was still in him, something that came out in childhood as disposition, as aspiration, and remained with him through the whole of his life on earth. In ancient times every oriental knew that what worked its way out of his soul during childhood, in youth, was a dowry from the spiritual worlds which he had experienced before entering into physical existence. To be aware theoretically that one has passed through a spiritual life of this kind before one's life on earth has no very great value, but a lively *feeling* for it is worth a great deal; it is something of the greatest value to feel that what has been growing and developing in one's soul since childhood comes from the spiritual world.

Today, however, this feeling has given way to another. It has given way, both in the individual and more especially in the social life, to another feeling entirely. And there is something important here which must be looked at. More and more there weighs down upon the human being, half unconsciously, the feeling of his inherited characteristics. Anyone who is able to view this impartially sees how the human being today actually feels that he is what he is through his parents, his grandparents and so on. Unlike the human being in ancient times he no longer feels that what flames up in him from childhood onwards, comes from those depths in which is rooted that which he received from his spiritual experiences before his life on earth. On the contrary he feels in himself the characteristics inherited from parents, grandparents and so on. The first thing people ask about a child nowadays is from whom it has got this or that characteristic. And the reply, however, is seldom that the child has it as a result of this or that particular experience in the spiritual world. People look instead to see whether it comes from the grandmother or grandfather, and so on.

The more this emerges in individual people – not merely as a theory but as a feeling, a feeling of dependence on purely earthly inherited characteristics – the more oppressive and dreadful will it gradually become. And this feeling will increase in strength very rapidly. In the decades ahead it will intensify to the point of becoming unbearable, for it is connected with another feeling, a certain feeling of the worthlessness of human existence. This will arise more and more: that the human being will feel his existence to be worthless if he cannot feel it to be anything other than the sum total of what has been implanted in his blood and in his other organs by physically-inherited characteristics. Today what is emerging here is still, to a certain extent, mere theory, although there are poets who have already expressed it as experience. But it will emerge as a feeling, as a sense, and it will then become an oppressive characteristic in the feeling-life of civilized humanity. This experiencing of oneself in the purely inherited characteristics will lie like a weight on the soul. It is here that the inability of natural science to give man an understanding of himself shows itself in all its poverty; the human being no longer feels himself to be a child of the spiritual world but merely a child of characteristics inherited in the course of earthly physical existence.

All this is very forcibly manifest in social life. You have only to think of the demands that have arisen as the outcome of a gigantic piece of political stupidity which has spread through the world in recent years! This folly slowly gathered strength during recent centuries and then came to a climax in our own day. The great crisis of the second decade of the twentieth century was ushered in when those who were supposed to be leading the several nations – who at any rate held positions which imply leadership and yet understood nothing of the situation mankind is in – when these people began talking about organizing mankind according to the will of its individual nations. It was indeed in our recent times that national chauvinism was aroused in its very worst sense. And it is national chauvinism that is ringing through the whole civilized world today.

This is merely the social counterpart of the utterly reactionary world-view that tries to trace everything back to inherited characteristics. When one no longer strives to fathom one's nature as a human being and to fashion the social structure in such a way that this human nature can be at home in it; and when one strives, instead, to bring it about that the social structure corresponds only with what men are as Czechs, Slovaks, Magyars, Frenchmen, Englishmen, Poles and so on, then one forgets all spirituality. Then all spirituality is excluded and people try to order the world solely in accordance with characteristics inherited through the blood because they have come more and more to the point of having no content at all in their concepts. This had to happen because this twentieth century had to give us a taste of the fact that there can be a man, marvelled at by vast numbers as a world-leader, even though there are no concepts in his words whatsoever – that there can be a man like Woodrow Wilson[2] who utters words which no longer contain any concepts.

It is for this reason that people have had to fall back upon something entirely devoid of spirit – on blood relationship, on the blood-related characteristics of the nations. All that has resulted from this is that peace treaties have been made in which people who know absolutely nothing about the conditions of life in the modern civilized world have determined the shape of the maps of the countries of that world. Nothing, perhaps, shows more clearly the materialism of modern times, its denial of everything spiritual, than the emergence of the principle of nationalism.

This, of course, is a truth which for many people today is highly unpleasant. And this is why so many lies have to be harboured in the deeper regions of the soul. For if one does not face honestly the fact that by establishing an order of the world based only on blood-relationship one is denying the spirit, then one is lying. And one is also lying when in such circumstances one then claims to be inclined towards some kind of spiritual conception of the world.

And now let us look at the way the evolution of the world is going today. Everything that is welling up out of the chaotic instincts of humanity denies the spirit utterly. I put you through a trial yesterday. In order to spare your delicate nerves, which I noticed yesterday to some extent, I will not add any more trials, although they could easily be added. Thus we see on all sides how man has lost insight into the true nature of his being. And let us now consider from a spiritual-scientific standpoint the counter-image of what I had to describe as a feeling that is surging up.

You know that spiritual science shows how our earth-planet, upon which the human being has to experience his present destiny, is the re-embodiment of three preceding conditions and how we have to look forward to three subsequent embodiments so that our earth, schematically, is in a midway state.

Now we know from what is described in my *Occult Science*³ that what the human being bears today as his physical body is essentially an inheritance from the first, second, third and fourth conditions. What he bears as his etheric body is a result of the second, third and fourth conditions. What we call his astral body is the result of the third and fourth conditions. And now, in our present earth-evolution, the 'I' is appearing. And there will appear in the future, when the earth enters its next stages, what today is indicated in the human being only in germ – spirit-self, life-spirit and actual spirit-man. These will have to be elaborated in the human being, just as physical body, etheric body and astral body have been elaborated, and just as the 'I' is being worked on at the present time.

But you will know, if you reflect on how much of this cosmic-earthly evolution can be brought to you, that during earth-evolution only the germs of spirit-self, life-spirit and spirit-man will be able to evolve; for we shall have to wait for the transformation of the earth into its three following conditions for them to appear fully. And from the descriptions I have given in my *Occult Science* you will see that, essentially, spirit-self is the transformation of the astral body into a higher stage, that life-spirit is the transformation of the etheric body to a higher stage and spirit-man is the transformation of the physical body to a higher stage. This transformation of the physical body, however, will not take place until the seventh condition – nor, correspondingly, the transformation of the other members.

Today, however, the human being can already understand that this has to happen. He can already embrace the *thought* that it must happen. Indeed, the human being can grasp still more today if, without prejudice, he gets beyond the limitations of natural science and directs his soul's gaze upon its own nature.

He will have to say to himself: 'It is true that, during earth-existence, I cannot attain spirit-self in my astral body, nor life-spirit in my etheric body nor spirit-man in my physical body, but what I have to do is to prepare, to prefigure, them in my soul. And by developing the consciousness-soul now I am preparing myself to take spirit-self into it in the next, the sixth, culture-epoch. I know that I cannot yet bring spirit-self into my entire astral body, but I have to bring it into my consciousness-soul. As a human being, I must learn to live inwardly in the way that I shall one day live when the earth has passed over, through a certain cosmic development, into its next stage of evolution. And I must prepare for these future conditions, at least inwardly, while still in earthly existence. I must prepare myself, in germ, inwardly so that in the future I shall be able to shape my outer form in the way which it is my task, even now, to understand.'

Now try and sense clearly what is really involved here. The human being is already growing into spirit-self, as I have often explained. The human being is growing into states of consciousness of which he must say that they are really of such a nature that, during the period of earth-existence, they cannot emerge fully. These states of consciousness try to transform him even as regards his external sheaths – his astral body, etheric body and physical body – but, as earthly man, he cannot achieve this. He has to say to himself: 'I must pass through the rest of earth-evolution continually feeling that I am preparing myself inwardly for conditions of being I cannot yet develop'. In future it will have to be the normal thing for a human being to say: 'I see the being of man as something which, in its inner nature, grows beyond what I can be as earthly man. As earthly man I am forced, in a sense, to feel myself as a dwarf compared with what the human being really *is*.' And out of this dissatisfaction, which properly educated children will begin to have in the very near future, this feeling will arise: The children will feel that, despite all our intellectual culture, people are still not able to solve the riddle of man. Man is missing from what can be known intellectually; he has no place in the social structure.

Everything that will develop out of the foolish Wilsonian formulas, and out of any other form of chauvinism that spreads over the world, will be quite unworkable. Through all such things modern civilization is heading towards impossible situations. However many more national states you set up you will provide only so many more seeds of destruction; and it is just out of everything that is loaded onto human souls as a result of modern civilization that the feeling I have just described from another point of view will proceed. The human being will say to himself: 'The being of man that lights up inwardly for me is something much higher than anything I can realize externally. I must bring something quite different to the world. I must bring something quite different into the social structure, something that is recognized as coming from spiritual heights. I cannot entrust myself to the social science derived from natural science.'

But the human being must sense the inner schism between his dwarf-like existence on earth and the experience that lights up within him of himself as a cosmic being. Out of all that modern culture – this much-praised, idolized culture of today – can give the human being, a twofold feeling will develop. On the one hand he will feel himself as belonging to the earth; on the other he will say: 'But the human being is more than an earthly being. The earth cannot fulfill the human being at all; if it *is* to fulfill him it will have first to transform itself into other conditions.'

In reality the human being is not an earth-being. In reality the human being is a cosmic being, a being belonging to the whole universe. On the one side the human being will feel himself bound to the earth; on the other he will feel himself to be a cosmic being. This feeling will weigh down on him. And when this is no longer mere theory but is experienced by individual human beings whose karma enables them to grow beyond the trivial feelings of today – when humanity comes to feel disgust at the thought of purely inherited characteristics and at the emotions engendered by chauvinism and turns against all this – only then will a kind of reverse begin. The human being will feel himself to be a cosmic being. As though with outstretched arms he will ask for the solution to the riddle of his cosmic being. This is what will come in the next decades: as though with outstretched arms – I mean this, of course, symbolically – the human being will ask: 'Who can decipher for me my nature as a cosmic being? Everything that I can establish on earth, all that the earth can give me, all that I can get from the natural science that is so highly valued today, accounts for me only as an earth-being and leaves the true being of man as an unsolved riddle. I know that I am a cosmic, a super-earthly being. Who can unravel for me the riddle of this super-earthly being?'

This will live in the human soul as a question rising up from a fundamental experience. In the decades to come, even before we reach the middle of this century, this question will be more important than anything else or any other feelings people may have. And the expectation, the longing, that there has to be a solution to this human riddle – the riddle that the human beings are, after all, cosmic beings. This feeling towards the cosmos – that one day it must reveal what cannot come from the earth – all this will create a mood to which the cosmos responds. Just as the physical Christ appeared at the time of the Mystery of Golgotha so the spiritual Christ will appear to humanity. He alone can give the answer because He is not in some indefinite place but must be recognized as a Being from beyond the earth who has united Himself with earthly humanity. People will have to understand that the question of cosmic man can be answered only if He who unites Himself with the earth from out of the cosmos comes to their aid. This will be the solution of the most significant disharmony that has ever arisen in earth-existence; the disharmony between the human being's feeling as an earthly being and his knowledge that he is a super-earthly being, a cosmic being. The fulfilment of this longing (*Drang*) will prepare man to recognize how, out of grey spiritual depths, the Christ-Being will reveal Himself to him and will speak to him spiritually, just as, at the time of the Mystery of Golgotha, He spoke to him physically.

The Christ will not come in the spirit if human beings are not prepared for Him. But they can be prepared only in the way I have just characterized, by sensing the discrepancy I described, by the schism weighing terribly heavily upon them from which they feel: 'I must regard myself as an earth-being. The intellectual development of recent centuries has created the conditions which make me appear as an earth-being. Yet I am no earth-being. I cannot but feel myself united with a being who is not of this earth; a being who, not with theological mendacity but in very truth can say: "My kingdom is not of this world".[4] For man will have to say to himself: 'My kingdom is not of this world.' And this is why he will have to be united with a being who is not of this world.

It is directly out of the sciences which, as I have said, will take possession of the popular consciousness with tremendous speed that something must be developed which will direct mankind towards the new manifestation of the Christ in the first half of the twentieth century.

This, of course, could not have happened in the constitution of soul in which the civilized world was before 1914 when all talk of ideals, all talk of spirituality, was fundamentally a lie. Deep need will have to make human beings' search for spirituality a true one. And the Christ will appear only to those who renounce everything that spreads falsehood over earthly life. And no social question will be solved that is not thought out in connection with this spiritual-scientific endeavour that enables the human being to appear in truth once again as a superearthly being. The solutions to our social problems will be found to the degree in which human beings are able to feel the Christ-impulse in their souls. All other solutions will lead only to destruction, to chaos. For all other solutions are based on the conception of man as an earthly being. But precisely in our own day the human being is outgrowing the constitution of soul which permits him to think of himself as a purely earthly, physical being. The new experience of the Christ will arise out of the attunement (*Gestimmtheit*) of human souls and out of their need.

But awareness must all the more be directed towards everything that hinders the approach of this new Christ-experience.

We had to refer directly to attacks on our own affairs and have seen that here also people take up an attitude towards the emerging spiritual science such that they fight against it out of an inner untruthfulness.

One experiences something in this area today which must be kept in view completely impartially. Almost every day at the moment spiritual science is, as it were, killed off at least once. The most recent of these death-blows was the one dealt by a theology professor, Karl Goetz, in agreement with another

Doctor of Divinity, a certain Heinzelmann.[5] I will disregard the fact that this Doctor of Divinity, Karl Goetz, has made an attack on spiritual science, or 'so-called spiritual science' as he terms it, for example in his newspaper article – we are having to get used to these things more and more here in Dornach. But one can also look from another point of view at everything that has been perpetrated by this Doctor of Divinity, Goetz. One can look at it from the point of view of how lacking in knowledge is this official erudition which has the education of contemporary youth in its care. One can deduce from this that there is an attack here on spiritual science. But one can look at the following, and I will highlight a few characteristic points – although only from the newspaper article – which, according to this attack, are supposed to occur. The methods of knowledge in spiritual science are referred to here by a man whose profession it is to speak about Christology, who gains his daily bread by educating youth in Christology. This man says, about the methods used to gain knowledge in anthroposophical science, that the Imaginations sought are the result of when the mental activity of forming ideas is artificially inhibited and suppressed. He says that the nervous energy saved in this way is then used to produce the mental images which anthroposophists call Imagination and Intuition.

So, just take a look at what this man says: Artificially constrained and repressed mental-picturing activity and, in the process, saved neural energy! One can disregard the fact that this man can of course only speak of saved neural energy as a vague hypothesis – for no one in science today can picture anything under the term of 'saved neural energy'. But he nevertheless talks of artificially constrained and repressed mental-picturing activity. Has this man in his 'scientific conscientiousness' – I choose the words carefully in this case and thus say in inverted commas, in his 'scientific conscientiousness' – ever really occupied himself with what, for example, is applied here as the methods of knowledge for coming to Imagination? Is it possible to speak here about constrained or repressed mental-picturing activity? Now, if he decided to look at some anthroposophical literature this man would be able to answer this. Those mental pictures which he considers to be his normal ones are indeed not repressed. Had he only tried a little to find out whether distorted mental pictures ruled the day while our School of Spiritual Science course was being held he would not speak about mental-picturing activity being suppressed here. There is still plenty of unsuppressed mental-picturing life here which, at least with regard to many a specialized science, is well able to understand what this man can understand. One simply cannot speak about suppressed mental-picturing activity [in this connection]. And if he had ever acquainted himself in his 'scientific conscientiousness' with what is described as the path into the spiritual worlds, he would have seen that nothing is artificially suppressed here but that things are freed. The case here is that this man has not understood a single word of what is contained in my book *Knowledge of the Higher Worlds – How is it Achieved?*. And he knows nothing of the methods of spiritual science other than what, in accordance with his constitution of soul, he can gather from the meditation successes of a bunch of old cronies. This is what is working under the name of 'scientific conscientiousness' in official science.

He goes on to say that through holding back these constrained mental pictures – people are supposed to imagine something here like mental pictures being dammed up like water – that, through this holding back, Imaginations come to life and appear like perceptions of the senses. Well, I would like to count up the pages where, again and again in my books, I have said that Imaginations have no similarity with pictures from the senses, with sense-perceptions. This is dealt with quite extensively. So what is ruling in this 'scientific conscientiousness'? The lie – which, albeit may arise from impotency, from inability. But this lie is spreading with tremendous speed in theology, philosophy, history, jurisprudence and similar branches of teaching. Modern humanity should take note of this fact. For it is in this fact – not in speeches that Woodrow-Wilsonism fabricates out of words empty of content – that the causes lie for steering us into chaos.

Then comes another good bit – as I said, I can only discuss this from the newspaper article. It says then that because these Imaginations, which have come to life through suppressing the mental-picturing element, arise involuntarily they are therefore described as being experiences free of the body. Again, in his 'scientific conscientiousness', he has never directed his mind to the fact that, as has been shown, nothing arises involuntarily but that in the spiritual-scientific act of knowing the voluntary mental picture is enhanced. Perhaps this man has got his information from a spiritistic or mediumistic nursery. If so, he should stay with his spiritism and mediums and keep away from things he does not understand and does not wish to understand.

And he says further that what personifies Imagination is that which is evoked through the split in consciousness. This is a lack of conscience and a twisting of everything that is portrayed in my books as the methods of knowledge of spiritual science! This man thereby prepares the ground in order to say, in his own way, that spiritual science may not be hostile towards Christianity, but is culturally valueless. And then comes the really good bit: spiritual science, he says, is culturally valueless for telepathy will never replace the telegraph, thought-reading will never replace the telephone nor magnetic healing-power replace medicine!

Thus, although during our course here at the Goetheanum we spoke about medicine and truly excluded all dilletantism about magnetic healing-powers, and although in truth we referred to medicine very seriously, a doctor of theology nevertheless gives a talk in our immediate neighbourhood after the course has ended about how the whole endeavour of spiritual science consists in trying to substitute medicine with magnetic healing-forces. And with this sort of talk a present-day doctor of theology enjoys success with the present-day public! And he enjoys success when a Heinzelmann-hobgoblin (see translator's note below) then jumps to his aid – a modern hobgoblin – and adds that one cannot find Christ through spiritual science but only through the Gospels. Now someone should just ask this hobgoblin: Which Gospel? One should ask him: What have you done to the Gospels with your theology? You have brought it about that the whole of Christology has vanished from modern development. And now that this mess has been created, we hear people from that corner saying: For Christianity we don't need what comes from spiritual science, we only need the simplicity of the Gospels. Is this not a most

---

Translator's note: In German *'Heinzelmannchen'* means goblin, brownie or imp. Steiner plays on this here in connection with the name of Professor Heinzelmann.

fundamental falsehood? It is a lie, knowing what modern criticism of the Gospels has come up with, to stand there and say: Our salvation for eternity must come from the Gospels without a science of the spirit.

What is it then that is coming from this corner? It is a denial of the Christ. And the most vigorous deniers of Christ today are the theologians. Those who want to prevent a true concept of the Christ from arising today are the theologians! And as long as it is not realized that this new experience of the Christ in the twentieth century will have to arise in such a way that the theology of all denominations denies him, the Christ will not come. He will appear again to human beings when those who are counted as his followers – the modern Scribes and Pharisees – have denied him completely.

It is not easy to see through these things with full strength, for one always also sees then how little the people of today are inclined to reckon with insights of this kind. The opponents are ready at their posts. They are developing all the intensity of battle. Our battle – what we are capable of – is weak, very weak and our comprehension of Anthroposophy is in many respects very sleepy. This is the great pain which weighs down these days upon someone who sees through things. One feels it so often when one says something in answer to the problems of our times – something for a social healing of our times – and people receive it as though it were barely anything other than a magazine article that was spoken rather than written. One would like to call upon people to awaken, to carry what can come from spiritual science into the way they shape all aspects of life. But, instead, one sees how people just let life run its course; how they look at those who direct life out of falsehood, and listen, greedy for entertainment, to what they receive from spiritual science as though it were nothing but a magazine article that was spoken rather than written. What must still arise is this: a deep, holy seriousness in receiving spiritual science and the disaccustoming of oneself from what induces people to receive spiritual science like any other literary product, albeit one in which one can amuse oneself all the better because it is a guarantee for one's longing for life after death. There is today a terrible gap between what is necessary in receiving spiritual science and what is actually there. You see, one can disregard an attack on Anthroposophy like that of Goetz or Heinzelmann. One has only to look at their abilities to ask: How was it that the pick of humanity was such that it brought these people to positions of this kind? Until one puts this question most intensely to oneself, until one is prepared to look where things are lacking, we will not make progress. All declaiming about social ideals or the like is useless if one is not prepared to look at this element that is living as a fundamental principle in our present time. For the damage of our time has its source in our perverted spiritual life which has gradually gone very deep into untruth but is completely unaware of how deeply in untruth it lives. How great is the contrast between what is necessary and the way in which what is spoken here is taken up! It is not intended to be a magazine article; it is meant as a force for life and people will have gradually to accustom themselves to understanding it as such.

This is what, in both a positive and negative sense, I wanted to say to you today concerning – to use a trivial word – the spirit of the age. This spirit of our age should be a spirit of expectation; the spirit which, out of expectation, develops an understanding for the great experience of the twentieth century that is born of deep need. But without also looking, in truth, at everything that is blocking this experience, people will not be able to meet it. If people today want, out of complacency, out of inner pleasure-seeking, to bow down to tradition – and if people do not want to be aware that, bowing down like this, they burden the day with a deep untruth – then people will not make themselves mature and ready for the Christ-event of the twentieth century. But everything depends on this maturity. Everything depends on our overcoming theological talk about Christ so that, in all reality, we can move forward to an understanding of Him.

NOTES

Lecture One

[1] These were the lectures given by Dr Karl Heyer on 14, 15 and 16 October 1920, during the first course of the School of Anthroposophy at the Goetheanum with the theme: 'The Science of History and History from the Viewpoint of Anthroposophy' ('Anthroposophische Betrachtungen über die Geschichtswissenschaft und aus der Geschichte'). These are printed in *Kultur und Erziehung* (the third volume of the *Courses of the School of Anthroposophy*), Stuttgart, 1921.

[2] See Wilhelm von Humboldt (1767–1835): *Über die Aufgabe des Geschichtsschreibers* (*The Task of the Historian*) in Volume IV of Humboldt's *Works* published by Leitzman, Berlin 1905 (see pages 35–56). Some relevant passages taken from these are as follows:

'The business of the historian, in the last but simplest analysis, is to portray the striving of an idea to attain existence in reality. For it is not always that it succeeds in this at the first attempt; and it is not so rare that the idea degenerates because it is unable to master in a pure way the matter counteracting it.'

'The truth of everything that happens lies in the addition of the above-mentioned invisible part of every fact, and thus the history writer must add this to the events. Seen from this angle he is self-acting and even creative – not, indeed, by producing what does not already exist, but by forming out of his own inner strength that which, as it is in reality, he could not perceive through mere receptivity. In different ways, but just like the poet, he must in himself transform the scattered fragments into a whole.'

'It may seem dubious to allow the realm of the history writer and that of the poet to meet, even at only one point. But the activity of both is undeniably related. For if the historian, like the poet, can achieve truth in his presentation of past events only by completing and linking the incomplete and disjointed elements of direct observation, then he does so, like the poet, only through imagination. Because, however, he places imagination subordinate to experience and the fathoming of reality, there is a difference here which cancels out all danger. Imagination does not work, at this lower position, as pure imagination, and is therefore more properly called an intuitive faculty and a talent for finding links.'

'Of necessity, therefore, the historian too, must strive; not, like the poet, to give his material over to the dominion of the form of necessity but to hold steadily in consciousness the ideas which are its laws, because, permeated only by these, he can then find their trace in the pure research of the real in its reality.'

'The historian encompasses all the threads of earthly activity and all varieties of supersensible ideas; the sum-total of existence, more or less, is the object of his work and he must therefore also follow all avenues of the mind and spirit. Speculation, experience and poetry, however, are not separate, opposed and mutually-limiting activities of the mind, but different planes of its radiance.'

'Apart from the fact that history, like every scientific activity, serves many subsidiary purposes, work on history is no less a free art, complete in itself, than philosophy and poetry.'

'Just as philosophy strives for the first foundation of things, and art for the ideal of beauty, so history strives for a picture of human destiny in faithful truth, living abundance and pure clarity that are perceived by the warm inner-being [of the historian] in such a way that his personal views, feelings and demands are lost and dissolved away. It is the final purpose of the history-writer to awaken and nourish this mood, which, however, he only attains when he pursues for his fellow human beings the simple presentation of past events with conscientious faithfulness.'

[3] See the final words of Rudolf Steiner, on 16 October 1920, after the close of the first course of the Anthroposophical School, in *Die Kunst der Rezitation und Deklamation* (First Edition) Dornach, 1928, page 118.

[4] See *Geschichtliche Symptomatologie* (GA 185), nine lectures given in Dornach in 1918, only two of which are translated in *From Symptom to Reality in Modern History*.

[5] See *Bedeutende Fördnis durch ein einziges geistreiches Wort* in *Goethes Naturwissenschaftliche Schriften*, edited and with a commentary by Rudolf Steiner in Kürschner's *Deutsche National-Literatur*, Volume II, page 34 (GA 1b). Goethe says here:

'I do not rest until I find a significant point from which a great deal can be deduced or, rather, which of its own will brings forth a great deal and presents this to me, and which I then, with attention and receptivity, work on further faithfully and carefully. If, in my experience, I find some phenomenon which I cannot deduce, I simply let it lie as a problem; and I have found, in my long life, this way of doing things to be very beneficial. For when I was not able for a long time to unravel the origin or connection of some phenomenon but had to put it to one side, I found that, years later, it all suddenly became clear in the most beautiful way.'

[6] Alcuin (also Alhuin or Alchwin, i.e. 'Friend of the Temple') was rector of the monastery school at York around 735 to 804. In 782 he followed the summons of Charlemagne and took on the headship of the court school. He encouraged the sciences in the monasteries and raised to the central seat of the sciences the monastery school of St Martin at Tours, which he founded and whose Abbot he became in 796.

The debate with the Greek is described in Karl Werner's book *Alcuin und sein Jahrhundert* (*Alcuin and His Century*) Vienna 1881, Chapter 11, page 166, as follows:

'Thus Charlemagne once wanted to know from Alcuin what should be made of the view of a Greek scholar, who presumably was a member of a Byzantine legation at Charlemagne's court, who had expressed the opinion to the emperor that Christ had paid the expiation for our sins to death. Alcuin found this manner of expression and the idea behind it to be inadmissible, for Christ was not death's debtor and could not become so – the price of our redemption was paid by Christ to our divine Father, to whom, in dying, He commended His soul. Death [so Alcuin argued] is in no way a reality of being and substance but, to his way of thinking, was something purely negative, the mere absence or 'Carence' (Church Latin: the interval before benefits become available) of life; it is nothing existing in itself, and thus cannot receive anything, no payment can be paid to it. On the contrary, in the person of Christ, death itself, which God did not create, became the ransom for our debt and won life for us thereby, which He Himself gives us in His saviour power.'

[7] Rudolf Steiner drew attention at different times to the fact that the content of the writings of 533 AD, attributed to Dionysius the Areopagite, do indeed stem from the person of this name mentioned in *The Acts of the Apostles* 17, 34). See the

lectures on 17 and 25 March 1907 in *Christianity Began as a Religion* and *Festivals of the Seasons* respectively.

[8] Johannes Scotus Erigena (c. 810–877) translator of the writings of Dionysius the Areopagite into Latin (see note 7).

[9] Nicolaus of Cusa (or Kures) (1401–1464), cardinal.

[10] Immanuel Kant [1724–1804]: *Critique of Pure Reason*, 1781; *Prologemena*, 1783.

[11] See Johann Gottlieb Fichte (1762–1814) *Erste und zweite Einleitung in die Wissenschaftslehre und Versuch einer neuen Darstellung der Wissenschaftslehre* (*First and Second Introduction into the Doctrine of Knowledge and an Attempt at a New Presentation of the doctrine of Knowledge*).

[12] *Grenzen der Naturerkenntnis* (*Limits to a Knowledge of Nature* (GA 322) – eight lectures given during the first course (*Hochschulkurs*) of the School of Spiritual Science in Dornach, 27 September to 3 October 1920 (GA 322).

[13] Baron Christian von Wolff, philosopher and mathematician, *Vernünftige Gedanken von Gott, der Welt und der Seele des Menschen, auch allen Dingen überhaupt*, 1719.

[14] David Hume (1711–1776), philosopher.

[15] Herbert Spencer (1820–1903), philosopher.

[16] John Stuart Mill (1806–1873), philosopher.

[17] See Rudolf Steiner, *Towards Social Renewal*, 1919, (GA 23).

[18] In the third week of the first course (of the School of Spiritual Science), Dr Carl Unger (1822–1929) gave lectures under the title of 'Rudolf Steiner's Works'. These six lectures, edited by Unger, can be found in Volume I of *Carl Unger's Writings*, Stuttgart, 1964.

[19] The first Goetheanum building, begun in 1913, was already put into use in 1920, although still under construction supervised by Rudolf Steiner and with the interior not yet finished. On New Year's Eve 1922–3 it was destroyed by fire.

[20] The Free Waldorf School was founded in Stuttgart in the spring of 1919 by Dr Emil Molt for the children, to begin with, of the employees of the Waldorf-Astoria cigarette factory. The school was under the supervision of Rudolf Steiner who appointed the teachers and gave the preparatory seminar courses.

[21] The first anthroposophical course of the Free School for Spiritual Science took place at the Goetheanum from 26 September to 16 October 1920. See also notes 1, 3, 12, and 18.

[22] I.e., a form of international support body for Waldorf Schools. Rudolf Steiner suggested the founding of a World Fellowship of Schools during an assembly of teachers on 16 October 1920. There is no available transcript of this talk.

Lecture Two

[1] See *Die soziale Grundforderung unserer Zeit – In geänderter Zeitlage*, twelve lectures, Dornach and Bern 1918, (GA 186).

[2] Karl Marx (1818–1883), founder of scientific socialism.

[3] Peter the Great (1672–1725), Tsar of Russia.

[4] Lenin, actually Vladimir Ilyich Ulyanov (1870–1924).

[5] Trotsky, actually Leib Bronstein (1879–1940).

[6] Cromwell's *Magna Charta Maritima* strengthened the position of the English fleet by decreeing that foreign goods could be imported only on English ships or ships of the country of origin. This measure struck a blow primarily at the Dutch hegemony in international carrying trade.

[7] Napoleon's decree from Berlin on 21 November 1806 imposed the strictest blockade of the British Isles by closing the entire Continent to trade and commerce with England.

[8] Alfred von Tirpitz (1849–1930), German Admiral of the Fleet and statesman, creator of the German naval fleet.

[9] See, *et al.*, the lectures from 20 to 22 January 1917, *Das Geheimnis des Lebens nach dem Tode* in *Zeitgeschichtliche Betrachtungen. Das Karma der Unwahrhaftigkeit, Zweiter Teil*, twelve lectures, Dornach 1917, (GA 174); *Individuelle Geistwesen und ihr Wirken in der Seele des Menschen*, nine lectures in different cities, 1917, (GA 178); and *Die okkulte Bewegung im neunzehnten Jahrhundert und ihre Beziehung zur Weltkultur*, thirteen lectures, Dornach 1915, (GA 254).

[10] In October 1920, professors and doctors of Oxford University sent an appeal to the professors of art and science in Germany and Austria, in order, as it says there, '... to remove the bitter enmity that has arisen under the influence of patriotism ...' and to find a reconciliation through the 'brotherly feelings of study' – article entitled *Die Völkerversöhnung (The Reconciliation of Peoples)* in the Basel *Nationalzeitung* of 20 October 1920.

Lecture Three

[1] Charles Darwin (1809–1882).

[2] In the year 869, the 8th Ecumenical Council of Constantinople under Pope Hadrian II, decreed, against Photios, that the human being has a rational and intellectual soul – *unam animam rationabilem et intellectualem* – so that it was no longer permitted to speak of a separate spiritual principle in the human being. The spiritual was henceforth seen more as a quality of the soul.

[3] Ignatius of Loyola (1491–1556), the founder of the Jesuit Order in 1534.

[4] Vladimir Sergeyevich Soloviev (1853–1900), Russian philosopher and poet.

[5] Rabindranath Tagore (1861–1941), Indian philosopher and poet.

[6] Albertus Magnus (1193–1280), Scholastic philosopher, called 'Doctor Universalis'.

[7] Thomas Aquinas (1225–1274), Scholastic and pupil of Albertus Magnus; called Doctor Angelicus. Canonized in 1323.

[8] Johannes Duns Scotus (1266–1294), Scholastic.

[9] Roger Bacon (1214–1294), Franciscan, taught at Oxford University.

[10] In the first Goetheanum. A presentation of the individual motifs of the small cupola can be found in *Der Baugedanke des Goetheanum (The Architectural Concept of the Goetheanum)*, Dornach, 1952.

Lecture Four

[1] See Rudolf Steiner's own review (GA 51) of his lecture to the Vienna Goethe Association (*Wiener Goetheverein*) on 27 November 1891 entitled *Über das Geheimnis in Goethes Rätselmärchen in den 'Unterhaltungen deutscher Ausgewanderter' (On the Secret in Goethe's Enigmatic Fairy Tale in 'Conversations of German Emigrants)* in *Literarisches Frühwerk*, Vol III, Book IV, Dornach, 1942. See also *Goethe's Standard of the Soul (Goethes Geistesart in ihrer Offenbarung durch seine 'Faust' und durch sein 'Märchen von der grünen Schlange und der Lilie')* (GA 22).

[2] See *On the Aesthetic Education of Man* published in 1795 in the *Die Horen*. This work arose from letters sent by Schiller to the Duke of Augustenburg between 1793 and 1795.

[3] Published in the *Die Horen* in 1795 as the close to the short story *Conversations of German Emigrants*.

[4] See *The Portal of Initiation – A Rosicrucian Mystery*, 1910, in *Four Mystery Dramas*, (GA 14).

[5] See Lecture One of this volume.

[6] See *Towards Social Renewal*, 1919, (GA 23). For what follows on here, see Chapter Two.

[7] See, for example, the conversation with Chancellor von Müller on 8 June 1830 and that with Eckermann on 11 March 1832.

[8] Herman Grimm (1828–1902). The quotations are from his essay '*Heinrich von Treitschke's German History*' (*Heinrich von Treitschkes Deutsche Geschichte*) in *Contributions to German Cultural History*, (*Beiträge zur Deutschen Kultur-geschichte*) Berlin, 1897, page. 5
[9] Erich Ludendorff (1865–1937), German general.
[10] Ralph Waldo Emerson (1803–1882), American writer and philosopher.
[11] Reference is made here to Oswald Spengler (1880–1936) and his work *Der Untergang des Abendlandes* (*The Decline and Fall of the Occident*), the first part of which was published in 1918.
[12] Arthur Drews (1865–1935), Professor of Philosophy at the Technical University at Karlsruhe, spoke on 10 October 1920 in lectures organized by the free religious congregation at Konstanz on 'Rudolf Steiner's Anthroposophy'. He repeated this lecture on 19 November in Mainz. His articles opposing Anthroposophy were published as a collection under the title *Metaphysik und Anthroposophie in ihrer Stellung zur Erkenntnis des Übersinnlichen* (*Metaphysics and Anthroposophy in their Position Regarding Knowledge of the Supersensible*), Berlin, 1922.
[13] Eduard von Hartmann (1842–1906), *Philosophie des Unbewussten: Versuch einer Weltanschauung* (*Philosophy of the Unconscious: An Attempt at a World-View*), Berlin, 1869.
[14] Count Hermann Keyserling (1880–1946). Compare, for example, the chapter '*Für und wider die Theosophie*' ('For and Against Theosophy') in *Philosophie als Kunst* (*Philosophy as an Art*), Darmstadt, 1920.

Lecture Five

[1] See *Das Ereignis der Christus-Erscheinung in der ätherischen Welt* (*The Event of the Reappearance of Christ in the Etheric World*), sixteen lectures given in different cities in 1910, (GA 118).
[2] Anatol Vasilevich Lunacharsky (1875–1933), Russian writer and politician. From 1917 he was the Commisar for the education of the masses.
[3] Karl Ferdinand Friedrich von Nagler (1770–1846).
[4] It has not been possible to establish who this was.

Lecture Six

[1] John Wyclif (c. 1324–84).
[2] John Huss (1369–1415).

Notes Lecture Seven – Disc 3

Lecture Seven

[1] August Weismann (1834–1914), German zoologist.
[2] Woodrow Wilson (1856–1924), President of the United States 1913–1921.
[3] *Occult Science*, (GA 13), published by Rudolf Steiner Press.
[4] 'My kingdom is not of this world' John: 18,36.
[5] Karl Goetz and Gerhard Heinzelmann – both theology professors at that time in Basel.